CAERPHILLY COUNTY BOROUGH

3 8030 08289 4265

D0993614

When FOOTBALL *Was* FOOTBALL

© Haynes Publishing, 2015

The right of Richard Havers to be identified as the author of this Work has been asserted
by him in accordance with the Copyright, Designs & Patents Act 1988.

All rights reserved. No part of this publication may be reproduced, stored in a retrieval system
or transmitted, in any form or by any means, electronic, mechanical, photocopying, recording
or otherwise, without prior permission in writing from the publisher.

First published in 2008

A catalogue record for this book is available from the British Library

ISBN 978-1-78521-024-2

Published by Haynes Publishing, Sparkford, Yeovil,
Somerset BA22 7JJ, UK
Tel: 01963 442030 Fax: 01963 440001
Int. tel: +44 1963 442030 Int. fax: +44 1963 440001
E-mail: sales@haynes.co.uk
Website: www.haynes.co.uk

Haynes North America Inc., 861 Lawrence Drive,
Newbury Park, California 91320, USA

All images © Mirrorpix

Designed for Haynes by BrainWave

Printed and bound in the US

When FOOTBALL Was FOOTBALL

A Nostalgic Look at a Century of Football

Richard Havers

Contents

When Football Was Football

Foreword by Steve Anglesey, editor Mirror.co.uk

"Millwall lost to Middlesbrough on Saturday by 2 goals to nil in the First Round of the English Cup…. Sandy Brown scored the 2 goals for the winners, of which one was freely considered an off-sider".
The Daily Mirror, February 8th, 1904.

You have just read the first ever – and possibly the briefest ever – football match report to appear in the Daily Mirror, which appeared under the headline 'Muddy Football Grounds and Heavy Going'.

Over a century later, we're still moaning about dodgy pitches and diabolical decisions. But so much else has changed, and not necessarily for the better.

Our beautiful game – the one the great Danny Blanchflower said was about about glory and doing things with style – has become a results-focused business, with an emphasis on physicality and speed over individual skill. Decaying old grounds and the hooliganism they bred have gone, but they have been replaced by sterile, biscuit-cutter stadiums where corporate customers are prized and huge sections sit in silence. Working-class fans and youngsters, once the lifeblood of the game, are being priced out of it. A generation is growing up with no experience of shouting for their local team in a cramped ground; why bother when you can watch your big four club every week from your front room?

This book is about a rougher but better time, before the satellite TV cameras, the prawn sandwiches and the £100,000-a-week salaries. It's about a time when the British appetite for football was just being whetted, when the Daily Mirror's innovative match reports and photography helped to spark the national pastime of football debate. An era when the football writer and the match photographer became the ears and eyes of the thousands of fans who couldn't get to the match.

Within these evocative images you'll find dirty shirts, team baths, lace-up boots, one-club men, supporters wearing flat caps and fedoras. And somewhere in the pages you'll find the real heart of our game.

Quite simply, this book is about a time when football was football.

The SIMPLEST GAME
1900-1920

Southend United players training in 1920.

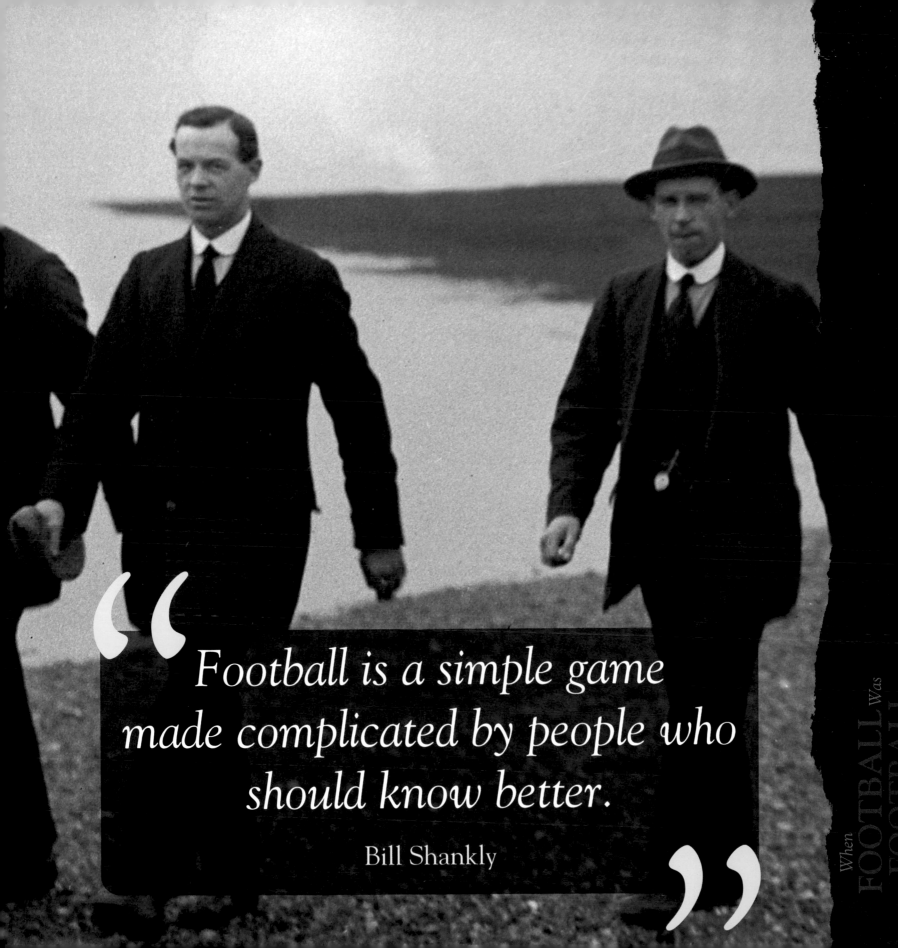

" *Football is a simple game
made complicated by people who
should know better.*

Bill Shankly "

1900 **Aston Villa** wins the first Football League Championships of the Twentieth Century. 1901 **Tottenham Hotspur** playing in the Southern League wins the FA Cup Final, the only non-league team ever to do so. 1904 Andy McCombie joins **Newcastle United** from **Sunderland** for £700. 1905 Alf Common the first £1000, transfer when he moves from **Sunderland** to **Middlesbrough**. 1907 The Professional Footballers Association is formed. 1908 Max Seeburg, a German, appears for **Spurs** and becomes the first foreign player in Britain. 1910 **Aston Villa** win league for a record 6th time. 1912 Danny Shea moves from **West Ham United** to **Blackburn Rovers** for £2,000. 1914 George V, the first reigning monarch to attend an FA Cup Final. **Bury** win the FA Cup twice. 1914 **Exeter City** became the first ever team to play a Brazil XI on a South American tour. 1914 Percy Dawson joins **Blackburn Rovers** for £2,500 from **Hearts**. 1914 The last FA Cup Final to be played at **Crystal Palace**. 1915 **Everton** win final league title before the outbreak of WW1. **Aston Villa, Newcastle United** and **Manchester United** the dominant teams during the first twenty years of the century. 1915 FA Cup Final was at Old Trafford. 1919 **Arsenal** join the First Division after it's reorganised, they've never left the top flight since. 1919 David Jack moves from **Plymouth Argyle** to **Bolton Wanderers** for £3,500. 1919 A £10 per week maximum wage for a footballer is established. 1920 Third Division is created. 1920 FA Cup Final at Stamford Bridge.

Prince Henry greets the Aston Villa team at the 1920 Cup Final at Stamford Bridge

The FA Cup 1900

In the Association Cup, as it was called at the turn of the century, Millwall from London, playing at home, managed to hold the mighty Aston Villa to a draw when they played in March 1900. Millwall made the semi final, no mean achievement given that they beat Aston Villa in the replay. Millwall went on to draw with Southampton at Crystal Palace in front of 35,000, but they then lost the replay. Southampton met Bury, another of the northern powerhouse teams, in the final but lost.

Aston Villa had the white sleeves while Millwall even then played in blue.

Millwall playing Southampton, in the stripes, at Crystal Palace.

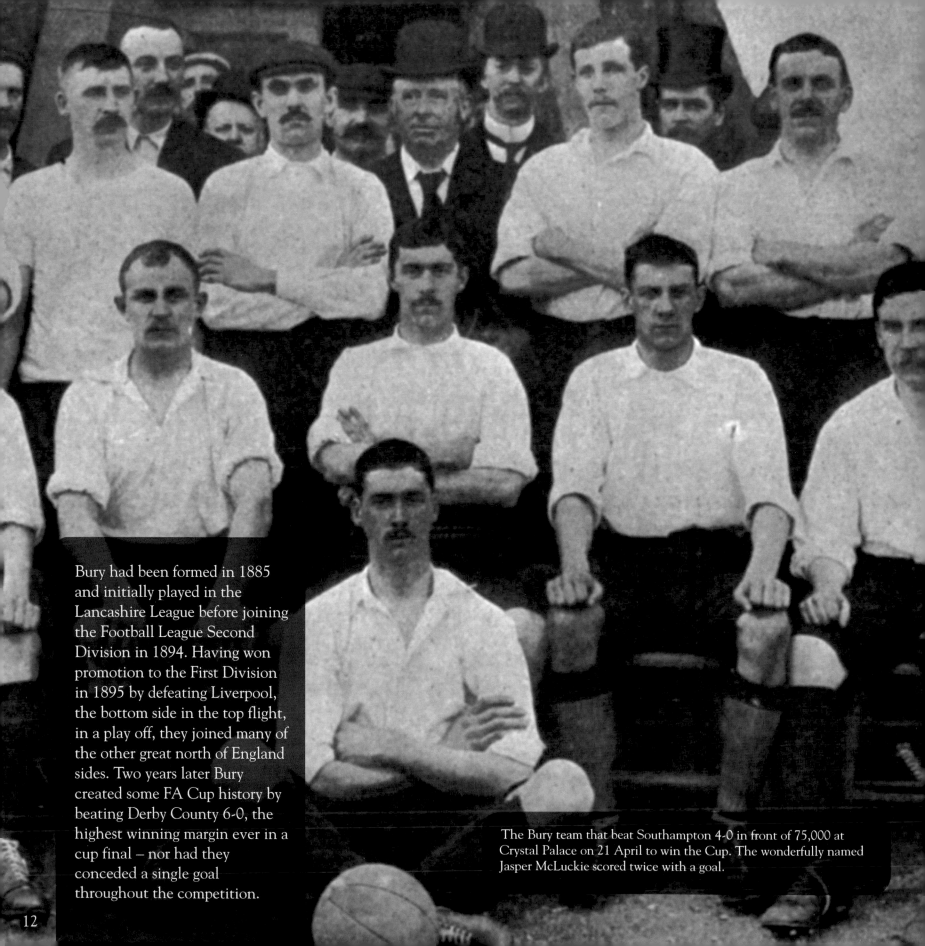

Bury had been formed in 1885 and initially played in the Lancashire League before joining the Football League Second Division in 1894. Having won promotion to the First Division in 1895 by defeating Liverpool, the bottom side in the top flight, in a play off, they joined many of the other great north of England sides. Two years later Bury created some FA Cup history by beating Derby County 6-0, the highest winning margin ever in a cup final – nor had they conceded a single goal throughout the competition.

The Bury team that beat Southampton 4-0 in front of 75,000 at Crystal Palace on 21 April to win the Cup. The wonderfully named Jasper McLuckie scored twice with a goal.

Football grounds in these pre radio and television days became ideal places for prospective parliamentary candidates to do a little electioneering. Conservative, Mr. A.J Balfour, he became Prime Minister in 1902, took the opportunity to kick off a match at Manchester City. In 1900 he's seen talking to the two opposing captains. The centre circle markings are very different to today's.

For most people amateur football remained their opportunity to both play or watch. This is Chester-le-Street AFC in 1900. Somewhere on this picture is a Mr. Wragg (of the horse racing family) and a Mr. Carr (of the biscuit making family).

The Mirror Covers Football

WOOLWICH TAKE THE FIELD.

In the first round of the English Cup Woolwich Arsenal met Fulham on Saturday on a wet and heavy ground. The Arsenal took the field a very fit team and well able, as the result proved, to realise the enthusiastic reception their supporters gave them.

MIDDLESBOROUGH v. MILLWALL.

Millwall lost to Middlesborough on Saturday by 2 goals to nil in the First Round of the English Cup. The Londoners were weak forward on account of the absence of Hulse and Moran, who were looking on, and J. H. Gettins was not in form. "Sandy" Brown scored the 2 goals for the winners, of which one was freely considered an "off-sider."

These are the first football photographs to appear in the Daily Mirror; both are from February 1904 and appeared on the same page of the paper. At the time much more prominence was given to the cup results than the league matches, which may have been due to the dominance of northern teams in the Football League First Division.

World Cup Winners

In 1911 All Durham Miners beat Juventus, Red Star and Stuttgart to win a competition organised by Sir Thomas Lipton. This is what the caption on the photograph in the archives says, but it seems that it was a little more complex than that.

Sir Thomas wrote to the football associations of Italy, Germany, Switzerland and England and asked them if they would like to send their best club side to Turin for an Easter tournament. Everyone accepted apart from England and from here the story becomes confusing. The story goes that Sir Thomas' secretary wrote to WAFC, somehow this letter got sent to West Auckland FC., rather than Woolwich Arsenal FC; although at the time Woolwich Arsenal were not the best club side in England, but then nor were West Auckland.

Whatever the truth a team from West Auckland went to Turin, it was mostly made up of miners who had to get the time off work to be able to play. West Auckland won their first game against Stuttgarter Sportfreunde of Germany and then played FC Winterhour of Switzerland, which the Durham side won 2-0. The King of Italy, Victor Emmanuel III and Sir Thomas Lipton presented West Auckland with the trophy after which the miners caught the train back to England.

–LEGENDS–

Billy Meredith

Billy Meredith, 'The Welsh Wizard', is the only player to have crossed the great Manchester divide from City to United and back again. Having been born in Wales he started out as a pit pony driver, while playing local amateur football. He joined Manchester City in 1894, shortly afterwards he scored twice in the Manchester derby against Newton Heath, who would soon become Manchester United; it sealed his reputation with the City fans and he became a huge draw.

In 1904 Meredith was accused of bribing an Aston Villa player and he received an eighteen-month ban from football. Upon his return he switched to United and made his debut against Villa in January 1907. He stayed with United until 1921 when he returned to City and carried on until his last game against Newcastle, one hundred and twenty days shy of his fiftieth birthday. In his latter days he continued to watch City rather than United where he was apparently made to pay for his tickets.

> *Football was my only love, for it is a noble and manly game.*
>
> Billy Meredith on his retirement

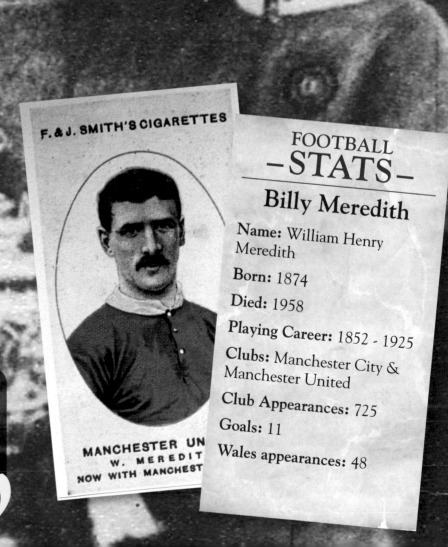

F. & J. SMITH'S CIGARETTES

MANCHESTER UN
W. MEREDIT
NOW WITH MANCHEST

FOOTBALL –STATS–

Billy Meredith

Name: William Henry Meredith

Born: 1874

Died: 1958

Playing Career: 1852 - 1925

Clubs: Manchester City & Manchester United

Club Appearances: 725

Goals: 11

Wales appearances: 48

ABOVE Billy Meredith training at Manchester United just before World War 1.

LEFT On 23 February 1924 Meredith, aged 49, played for Manchester City against Brighton & Hove Albion; City won 5-1 with Meredith scoring following a corner, making him the oldest player to have scored in the FA Cup.

17

League football was suspended in July 1915 as more and more men volunteered to fight. The 17th Battalion of The Middlesex Regiment was even known as the 'Footballers' Battalion' because of the large number of former footballers in its ranks. These are members of the Army Service Corps in France in 1915 playing in their time away from the front.

With little football being played at the major football grounds some were converted into makeshift factories. Tottenham Hotspurs' ground, White Hart Lane, was just off the High Road in Tottenham and was formerly the site of a market garden.

This factory was used to make gas masks and other protective equipment and almost all the workers were women. The pictures, taken in July 1916, show them at their workbenches and some of the women modeling the leather hoods with the eyeholes cut out.

NEW REVELATIONS AT THE SPY TRIAL IN PARIS

The Daily Mirror

CERTIFIED CIRCULATION LARGER THAN THAT OF ANY OTHER DAILY PICTURE PAPER

No. 4,944. Registered at the G.P.O. as a Newspaper. MONDAY, SEPTEMBER 1, 1919 [16 PAGES.] One Penny.

HEIR'S £5 A WEEK JOB | THE ASSOCIATION SEASON OPENS

Cornelius Vanderbilt, a son of Brigadier-General Cornelius Vanderbilt, who has forsaken his holiday to become a "cub" reporter on the New York *Herald*. The heir to millions, he will receive a salary of £5 a week. "I wanted to be a reporter," he said, "because I have always found newspaper men to be the most alert people I know."

Holt, the South Shields goalkeeper, clearing in the match against Fulham.

Lawrence, the Newcastle United goalkeeper, punches away. The United scored the only goal

Groves, of the Arsenal, falls after making a shot in the match against Newcastle United at Highbury.

Boyne (left) scores for Brentford against Brighton and Hove.

The Association football season opened on Saturday with a full programme of matches in both English and Southern Leagues. The various teams received a warm welcome from large crowds, and though, of course, there is an element of uncertainty about the early games, they provided plenty of excitement.—(*Daily Mirror* photographs.)

1919 – *The Victory Season*

The opening day of the 1919/20 football season, the Victory season, got underway on 30 August and was front page news on the Daily Mirror. Throughout the war former professional footballers played wherever they could get a game; some for teams close to where they were stationed, while those at the front kicked a ball whenever time allowed.

With the war to end all wars over the anticipation surrounding the new season was immense, although no one quite knew what to expect from the teams in the first division. Practice matches had been held the previous Saturday and the paper claimed that the astute managers had been building their sides back up from the time of the Armistice. The opening fixtures included Arsenal at home to Newcastle, Sunderland against Aston Villa and the only other London club in the top flight, Chelsea, away to Everton.

GREAT RUSH TO LEAGUE MATCHES.

Half a Million People Present at Thirty-Three Games — Unparalleled Enthusiasm.

Never has a football season opened more auspiciously than did that of 1919-20. Packed grounds were the order on Saturday, and the fact that the nimble-sixpence has given place

settled down to play the football one expected of them. Play by certain individuals was excellent, but we saw little of the famous combination which is a tradition of the Newcastle men or of the good understanding which usually prevails among the

"The weather was perfect for the opening. A good breeze tempered the rays of the late summer sun. In fact there was a decided reminder of autumn in the air." Is how the report on the season's opening day began. 258,000 fans watched the eleven First Division games, while 155,000 watched the Second Division games. Elsewhere in the paper there was an article highlighting the fact that "thousands of women now attend football matches, whereas hundreds did so before. They look forward to an outing with a husband or a sweetheart and understand and enjoy the game."

At the time the winning team was always put first in the results rather than the home side. With far fewer southern teams in both of the top two divisions the Southern League Division 1 was where many of the names familiar to us today were playing.

SATURDAY'S FOOTBALL RESULTS AT A GLANCE.

LEAGUE—Div. I.		LEAGUE—Div. II.		SOUTHERN LEAGUE—Div. I.	
Blackb. R. (h) 4	Preston N.E. 0	Birmingh. (h) 4	Hull City 1	Brentford (h) 2	Brigh. and H. 1
Derby Co. (h) 1	Manchester U. 1	Blackpool (h) 4	Leeds City 2	Crystal Pal (h) 2	Northampton 2
Manch. C. (h) 3	Sheffield U. 3	Fulham (h) 1	South Shields 0	Gillingham (h) 0	Watford 0
Notts Co. (h) 2	Burnley 0	Huddersfield (h) 2	Clapton Orient 1	Luton (h) 1	Swansea T. 1
Sunderland (h) 2	Aston Villa 1	Stoke (h) 2	Barnsley 0	Norwich (h) 4	Newport Co. 1
West Brom. (h) 3	Oldham Ath. 1	W. Ham U. (h) 1	Lincoln City 1	Plymth. A. (h) 3	Swindon 0
Chelsea 3	Everton (h) 2	Stockport Co. 3	Grimsby (h) 0	Reading (h) 2	Cardiff 0
Middlesbrough 1	Sheffield W. (h) 0	Wolverh. Wan. 2	Leicester C. (h) 1	Queen's P. R. 2	Bristol R. (h) 0
Newcastle U. 1	Arsenal (h) 0	Tot'en. Hotspur 5	Coventry C. (h) 0	Portsmouth 2	Southnd. U. (h) 0
Liverpool 3	Bradford C. (h) 1	Bristol C. (h) 1	Bury 0	Southamp. (h) 1	Exeter City 1
Bradford 2	Bolton W. (h) 1	Rotherh. C. (h) 2	Notts Forest 0	Millwall 2	Merthyr (h) 0

SCOTTISH LEAGUE.—Aberdeen (h) 1 Clyde 0 Airdrie 1   ASSOCIATION MATCHES.—Sutton United (h)

Back row, left to right: Colin Myers, George Nicholls and Andrew Newton. Front row: Robert Reid and Tom Capper.

SOUTHEND ON SEA

In 1920 most of the teams in the old Southern League were formed into the Third Division South, a year later the Third Division North came into being. One of the founding twenty-two teams in the southern division was Southend United – the aptly named Shrimpers. The club never gained promotion from the Third Division South and became part of the restructured Third Division in 1958, where they remained until 1966 when they were relegated to the Fourth Division. These photographs show some of Southend's players training for their cup tie; all the effort paid off because they beat Second Division, Blackpool 1-0.

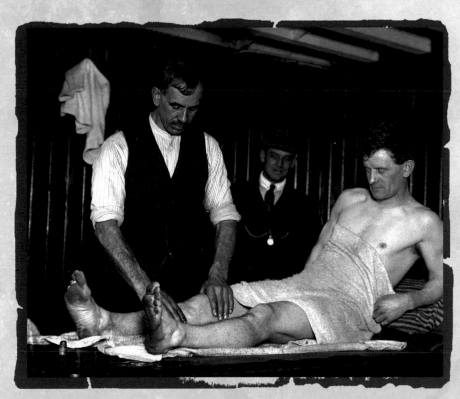

Jack Campbell massaging Joe Walter.

Left to right Joe Dorsett, Tommy Nuttall and Joe Walters.

Captain, Arthur Whalley.

ABOVE Prince Henry meets the Huddersfield team.

LEFT The captains, Andy Ducat of Villa and Fred Bullock of Huddersfield.

The FA Cup 1920

This was the first cup final for five years and according to the match report, "It was quite an average final." Aston Villa won by a goal to nil in extra time of the game, which was played at Stamford Bridge. It was watched by just 50,000 people – considered a very small crowd at the time. This was the sixth time that Villa had won the FA Cup, but it would be their last time for thirty-seven years.

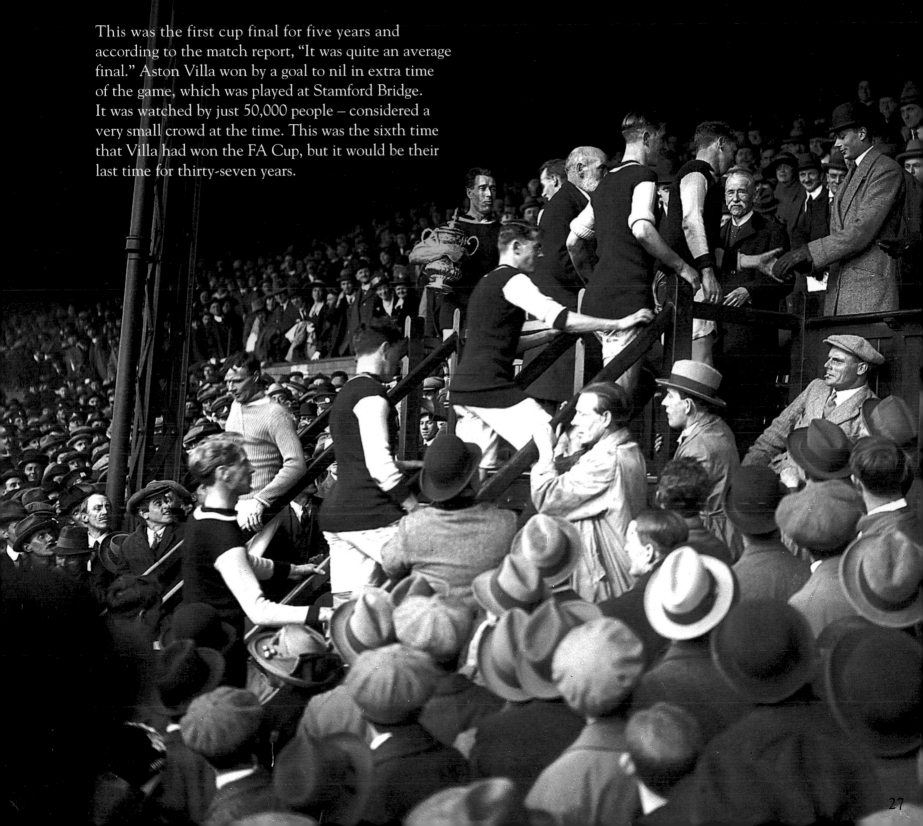

TOUGH GAME

1921-1945

> " *To think of football as merely 22 hirelings kicking a ball is merely to say that a violin is wood and cat-gut, Hamlet so much ink and paper. It is conflict and art* "
>
> J.B. Priestley

England played the Rest of Europe at Highbury in October 1938.

1921 Third division north and south are created as the Football League expands to be 92 clubs. 1923 First Wembley cup final. 1922 Sid Puddefoot £5,000 from **West Ham** to **Falkirk.** 1923 **Belgium** are the first foreign team to avoid being defeated by England; it was a 2-2 draw. 1926 **Huddersfield** become the first team to win the league three times in succession. 1927 **Cardiff** became the first non-English club to win the FA Cup final. 1928 Dixie Dean scored 60 league goals in a season for **Everton**. 1928 **Chelsea** and **Arsenal** become first teams to play with shirt numbers. 1928 David Jack moves from **Bolton** to **Arsenal** for £10,890. 1930 The first 6-6 draw in football league, it's between **Leicester & Arsenal**. 1931 **Aston Villa** set an all-time League Division 1 record of 129 goals in a season, but still finish runners-up to **Arsenal**. 1931 **Arsenal** become first London team to win the league. 1931 Billy Richardson of **West Bromwich** Albion scored five times in the first five minutes against **West Ham**, they won 5-1. 1934 84,569 watched **Manchester City** beat **Stoke City** at Maine Road, the biggest football league crowd outside of Wembley. 1934 **Manchester United** saved from relegation to the 3rd Division North by beating **Millwall** 2-0. 1935 **Arsenal** wins third successive League Division one title. **1937** First FA Cup Final to be televised. 1938 **Arsenal** win the league but only finish with 16 more points than the bottom club **West Bromwich Albion**. 1938 Bryn Jones moves from **Wolves** to **Arsenal** for £14,000. 1938 First penalty awarded in FA Cup at Wembley. 1939 League is abandoned three games into the season with the outbreak of the Second World War.

Chelsea play Moscow Dynamos at Stamford Bridge in 1945; 100,000 are thought to have attended.

ENCLOSURE
STANDING ONLY .9ᴰ

B...
of
PICKPOCKE

The Charity Shield

In 1898 the Sheriff of London's Shield was introduced as a competition for players v gentlemen - the professionals versus the amateurs. The Football Association Charity Shield replaced it in 1908 after the amateur clubs fell out with the Football Association. The first game was between the winners of the first division, Manchester United and the winners of the Southern League, Queens Park Rangers; after a drawn game United won the replay 4-1. After various other permutations of participants the winners of the FA Cup, Tottenham Hotspurs, played the winners of the league, Burnley at Stamford Bridge in 1921 – Spurs won 2-0.

CHAOS AT CUP-TIE FINAL: WHO WAS TO BLAME?

The Daily Mirror

NET SALE MUCH THE LARGEST OF ANY DAILY PICTURE NEWSPAPER

24 PAGES

No. 6,079.

Registered at the G.P.O. as a Newspaper.

MONDAY, APRIL 30, 1923

One Penny.

POLICE v. CROWD: WEMBLEY'S FIRST CUP FINAL

A remarkable photograph, taken from the air, of the Stadium at Wembley, with spectators swarming over the playing pitch, while hundreds are clustered outside.

Arnold Ratcliffe, of Bolton. He was crushed and picked up unconscious.

Thomas McGrigor, of Islington, in hospital with a broken arm and leg.

Official records will claim that the first contest to be staged at the Empire Stadium, Wembley, was the final for the Football Association Challenge Cup between West Ham United and Bolton Wanderers. The many thousands who journeyed to Wembley on

Saturday will, however, long retain the memory of an earlier struggle in which the opposing elements were police and public, the ultimate victory resting with the force, whose untiring efforts eventually produced order from utter chaos.

The First Wembley FA Cup Final

The first Wembley Cup Final was one marred by injury to hundreds of spectators. There were immediate calls for an enquiry into how 100,000 spectators seemed to swarm out of control and force open the gates. It was estimated that there were 200,000 people in Wembley, which at the time was designed to accommodate 125,000. The game between Bolton Wanderers and West Ham United kicked off forty-five minutes late as the police struggled to control the crowds. Such was the overcrowding that in order to take a corner police had to clear a run up for the player taking the kick. Bolton won 2-0.

–LEGENDS–

Herbert Chapman

Herbert Chapman like many football managers had been a player, but his was an undistinguished playing career. He first became a manager in 1908 for Northampton Town, who was in the Southern League, before he switched to Leeds City. He made steady progress with the club before the war intervened. He was then caught up in a scandal, which gave rise to Leeds City being disbanded and Chapman himself briefly banned. He successfully appealed and took over as Huddersfield manager, leading them to two League titles and an FA Cup win. In 1925 Chapman was lured to London by Arsenal, they doubled his salary to £2,000, and he transformed the previously unsuccessful team into FA Cup winners in 1930 and League winners in 1930/31 and again in 1932/33. Chapman built his Arsenal team by big spending coupled with judicious bargain buys. Outside of football perhaps his best move was to get the London Transport Passenger Board to change the name of Gillespie Road underground station to Arsenal. In 1934 Chapman died at his desk in his office at Highbury.

Arsenal in 1927.

> "*Arsenal's status as one of the world's top football clubs is very largely the legacy of one man, Herbert Chapman.*"
>
> Stephen Studd
> (Chapman's biographer)

FOOTBALL –STATS–

Herbert Chapman

Name: Herbert Chapman

Born: 1874

Died: 1934

Playing Career: 1895 - 1909

Clubs: 11 in all including Tottenham Hotspur and Northampton Town

Club Appearances: 100+

Goals: 40+

Managerial Career: 1807 - 1934, Northampton Town, Leeds City, Huddersfield Town and Arsenal

Golfing Footballers

Golf has been a popular game among footballers for a long time, although in more recent times it's probably on the wane. In April 1924 the Daily Mirror hosted a foootballer's golf competition at Hadley Wood in Hertfordshire. The clubs entered teams; Spurs had three, Arsenal two and Fulham one, along with some individual players.

TOP Bob Turnbull (Arsenal), Frank Osborne (Spurs), Bert Smith (Spurs), W. Field (Q.P. Rangers), Charlie Walters (Spurs), W. Sage (Spurs).

ABOVE Billy Milne (Arsenal), Alf Baker (Arsenal), J. Ross (Spurs), R. Macdonald.

LEFT Tommy Clay (Spurs) & Tom Whittaker (Arsenal)(Spurs).

The 1925 FA Cup Final

Sheffield United have won the FA Cup four times, the last time being in 1925 when they beat Cardiff City 1-0, it also marked the first time that a team from outside England appeared in the final. It was seen as a patriotic win as the paper ran with the headline, "Welsh Soccer Invasion repelled At Wembley" and "Sheffield United Defend The English Cup." Cardiff were lying thirteenth, one place above Sheffield United, in the First Division.

Sheffield United, like most teams at the time travelled by train to London and this was them on their return north at Liverpool Station. Captain Billy Gillespie who played almost 500 games for the Blades and scored 137 goals is seen holding the cup. On the front right of the picture is Fred Tunstall who played for United for eleven years and was instrumental in them winning the cup. Not only did his great shot win the final, but he scored twice in the semi final against Southampton, his only goal of the game beat Everton in the fourth round and he scored one of United's two goals against West Bromwich Albion in round four.

SHEFFIELD UNITED'S TRIUMPH IN THE CUP FINAL—WON BY THE

The Duke of York shaking

Gillespie, the Sheffield captain,

Tunstall, slipping between two C

Sutcliffe, Sheffield's goalkeeper, leaping amid a crowd of players to punch away a corner kick during the Cup final at Wembley.

YACHT OWNER'S ESCAPE.—The yacht Maid, Marion which, while anchored off Ryde, was in collision with a mailboat and sank. The owner, Mr. J. Ray Sand and his wife, who were asleep on board, escaped in their night clothes.

VETERANS' RACE.—Shaun Spadah and Music Hall taking a fence neck and neck at Sandown on Saturday. Shaun Spadah, however, won by ten lengths, after leading for most of the distance.

THE KING'S HOME-COMING.—The King greets the Duchess of York the Duke, on their Majesties return from the Continent. Princess Mary is left, Prince George, Prince Henry and Viscount

There were 91,763 people at Wembley Stadium, but unlike two years earlier everything went off calmly, with no repeat of the unruly crowd scenes.

Bolton player Jimmy Seddon, holding the trophy, Billy Butler (on left) and Ted Vizard.

The 1926 FA Cup Final

The FA Cup Final at Wembley on 24 April 1926 between Bolton Wanderers and Manchester City was the first to be broadcast on the radio - in fact the first tie in any round. It was not a broadcast that everyone in Britain could hear, even if they owned a wireless, as it was only relayed to public halls in Bolton and Manchester. Bolton won 1-0 with a goal by David Jack. This was expected to be the last Wembley Cup Final as it was due to be sold.

TOP RIGHT Jimmy McMullan (left) of Manchester City and Joe Smith of Bolton before the game. McMullan went on to become Aston Villa's first manager in 1934; up until then the team had been selected by a committee.

RIGHT Dick Pym, the Bolton keeper goes down at the feet of a City player. Pym won three FA Cup Winner's medals with Bolton and lived to be 95 years old.

James holds the FA Cup aloft after beating Sheffield United in the 1936 FA Cup final at Wembley.

–LEGENDS– Alex James

Alex James was an inside forward and his passing skills and ball control were fabulous despite the fact that he was plagued by rheumatism; this necessitated him wearing baggy shorts to hide his 'long johns'. Born in Lanarkshire his first club was Raith Rovers whom he joined in 1922 and stayed with them until his move to Preston in 1925. In 1929 Herbert Chapman paid £8,750 to lure him to Arsenal where he remained for the rest of his career.

  With the £8 per week maximum wage Arsenal got around this by paying James, £200 per year as a 'sports demonstrator' at a London department store. For Arsenal his role was to play deep, so his goal scoring was less prolific than it had been with his previous clubs. It was as a provider that he excelled and Arsenal's success during the early thirties had a great deal to do with Alex James' distribution and vision. He retired aged thirty-six having struggled with numerous injuries; he served in World War Two with the Royal Artillery, became a journalist and died of cancer in 1953.

ABOVE Alex James with his teammate Joe Hulme who is attempting to untangle himself from a police officer who is guarding the cup.

FOOTBALL
–STATS–

Alex James

Name: Alexander Wilson James

Born: 1901

Died: 1953

Playing Career: 1922 - 1937

Clubs: Raith Rovers, Preston Noth End & Arsenal

Club Appearances: 476

Goals: 116

Scotland appearances: 8, Goals 3

Wembley Stadium shortly after the kick-off of the 1927 Cup Final between Arsenal and Cardiff City.

The FA Cup Leaves England 1927

The Final between Cardiff City and Arsenal was historic because the Welsh team won; for the first time the FA Cup left England, but it was also the first match to be broadcast to the nation on the wireless. Both teams were mid-table in Division One although Arsenal was 11th, three places above Cardiff. Having narrowly lost to Sheffield United two years earlier by 1-0 they inflicted a similar fate on Arsenal. It would be the last time for 61 years that any team other than an English team competed for the FA Cup at a final – in 2008 Cardiff were back at Wembley but lost to Portsmouth. Perhaps inevitably, by 1-0.

Cardiff City fans watching the changing of the guard at Horse Guards Parade in Whitehall.

Cardiff's Billy Hardy beats Arsenal's captain Charlie Buchan to a cross.

Cardiff keeper Tom Farquharson leaps to clear an Arsenal attack. Left to right: Tom Watson, Charlie Buchan, Billy Hardy, Tom Farquharson, Tom Sloan, Sam Irving, Fred Keenor, Jimmy Brain.

Mr T.P. Ratcliffe conducts the crowd before the game with the band of the Grenadier Guards. This was the first time that community singing was introduced at the Final and 'T.P.' did every final up until the Second World War.

Cardiff City captain Fred Keenor, holding the FA Cup, leans out of the window as the rest of the team struggle to reach the bus.

The Cardiff City team. Back row, left to right: George Latham (trainer), Jimmy Nelson, Tom Farquharson, Tom Watson, George McLachlan. Middle row: Tom Sloan, Sam Irving, Fred Keenor (captain), Billy Hardy, Len Davies. Front row: Ernie Curtis, Hughie Ferguson.

> " *The reason women don't play football is that eleven women would never wear the same outfit in public.* "
>
> Phyllis Diller

Ladies football was by no means new in the 1920s; matches had been taking place for many years, although the Football Association barred women from playing at the best grounds in 1921. By the time this match took place in 1928 women's football was waning fast. Representing England were Bradford's Hey's Brewery and Scotland had Kellys.

Heys Brewery.

Kellys XI with their mascot.

In the 1929 FA Cup Final Bolton Wanderers beat Portsmouth 2-0;
Fred Forward, Portsmouth outside right, tackled by Alec Finney,
Bolton's left back (white shirt).

1930 *FA Cup Final*

When Arsenal played Huddersfield on 25 April 1930 it was not so much the result that made this final so well remembered as the image of the German Graf Zeppelin flying low over Wembley Stadium. The airship, the largest ever built by that time, cast its sinister image over the ground and was booed by some of the crowd who thought it might distract the players.

Arsenal won 2-0 and their goals came from Alex James and Jack Lambert. Because Herbert Chapman had previously managed Huddersfield both teams came out onto the pitch walking side by side. Arsenal's victory meant that this was only the third time the cup had come to London since 1882. British Movietone News filmed the match and showed it in cinemas throughout England on the Monday following the game.

Arsenal with its' big-spending manager had earned the nickname 'The Bank of England Team'. Hugh Turner, the Huddersfield keeper dives but fails to stop Arsenal scoring.

The FA Cup Final
1932

This was Arsenal's third appearance in the final in six years and the second time they had been the losing side, although this time it was in somewhat controversial circumstances. Arsenal's Bob John had given them the lead but Newcastle equalised after the ball had appeared to have gone out for a goal kick; Newcastle's Jimmy Richardson crossed the ball back into the goalmouth for Jack Allen to equalise. Allen added a second goal and Newcastle won the cup for the third time in their history. Later photographs proved the ball had gone out of play, but of course the goal stood causing Arsenal fans for many years to refer to this as the 'Over the Line' final.

Frank Moss, the Arsenal keeper, rushes out to intercept a ball that Jack Allen, the Newcastle centre forward, is chasing.

Crowds surrounding Newcastle football team's cars at King's Cross station the day before the final.

Arsenal football team and officials board an Imperial Airways flight at Croydon – London's main airport – in October 1932 en route to Paris to play the Paris Racing Club in a charity game; all the monies raised being donated to war invalids. The following day there was an article in the Mirror suggesting that instead of travelling by train, Plymouth Argyle, who were in Division Two, would travel by air thanks to their President who was to 'engage an airliner to convey them to all away Second Division matches'.

Arsenal started their defence of their First Division title in 1933 with a home game at Highbury against Birmingham City; it ended 1-1 and Arsenal finished the season three points ahead of Huddersfield Town with Spurs a distant third.

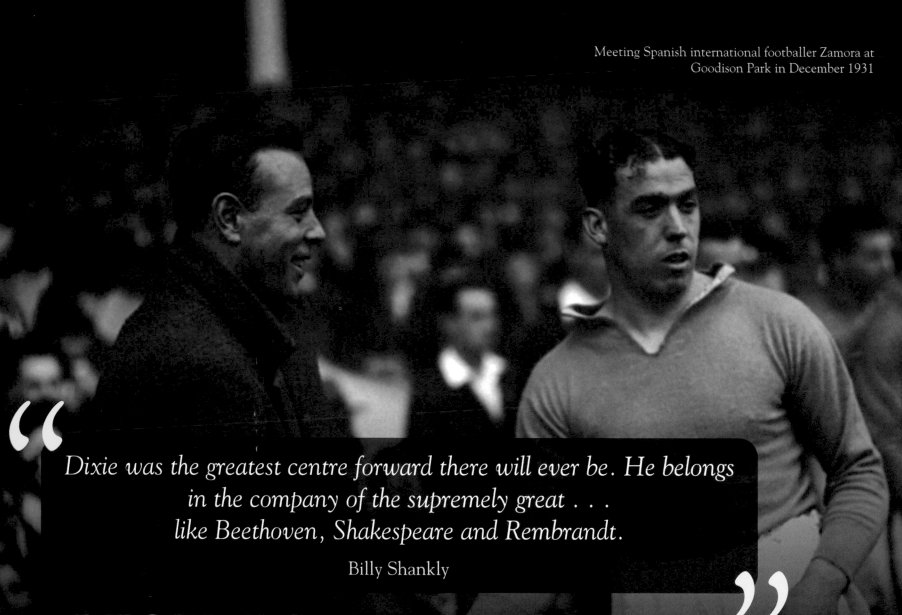

> *Dixie was the greatest centre forward there will ever be. He belongs*
> *in the company of the supremely great . . .*
> *like Beethoven, Shakespeare and Rembrandt.*
>
> Billy Shankly

–LEGENDS– Dixie Dean

No one in English football deserves the epithet 'goal machine' more than Dixie Dean; his career tally left him not far short of a goal a game. It's said he got his nickname because of his dark complexion and curly hair, comparing him to Black people in the US Southern States; he never liked it and preferred to be called Bill.

Everton signed him from Tranmere Rovers for £3,000 in 1925 and his impact was immediate, scoring 32 goals in one season. The following year he suffered a serious motorbike accident but fully recovered to score 60 goals in the 1927/28 season. When his playing career ended he ran the Dublin Packet in Chester and worked as a porter at Littlewoods Football Pools. He died watching his beloved Everton play Liverpool in 1980 and in 2001 a statue was erected at Goodison Park with the inscription 'Footballer, Gentleman, Evertonian'. A fitting tribute to a man who was often at the centre of the very roughest tackles, yet was never booked or sent off.

FOOTBALL
-STATS-

Dixie Dean

Name: William Ralph Dean

Born: 1907

Died: 1980

Playing Career: 1923 - 1939

Clubs: Tranmere Rovers, Everton, Notts County and Sligo Rovers

Club Appearances: 484

Goals: 419

England appearances: 16, Goals 18

Bill Dean seen here in 1950 behind the bar of 'The Dublin Packet' with his England caps.

Preparing for the FA Cup Final. The improvement to the seats in the new Wembley Stadium compared to these hard wooden benches is most welcome.

The 1934 FA Cup Final

Manchester City won the FA Cup in 1904 but since then has twice been on the losing side; in 1926 and again in 1933 against Everton, when Dixie Dean scored twice in a 3-0 win. Much of the match was played in a thunderstorm and in the 28th minute the delightfully named Septimus Rutherford put Portsmouth ahead due to a goal-keeping error by Frank Swift, the 20-year-old City keeper. At half time Swift was still blaming himself for the error but Fred Tilson, the City No. 11 said, 'Don't worry, I'll plonk two in next half'. And he did, in the 74th and 88th minutes after Portsmouth had lost Jimmy Allen, their defender, through injury and were reduced to ten men – this was long before substitutes were allowed.

Swift (pictured right) went on to become one of England's greatest keepers, although the Second World War robbed him of some of his best years. He was tragically killed in the Munich air disaster after reporting on Manchester United's match.

England v Germany – 1935

The German goalkeeper, Jacob, watched by George Camsell (far right) against England at White Hart Lane on 4 December 1935. George Camsell only played nine times for England, but scored 18 goals; he spent most of his career at Middlesbrough and scored 345 times in 453 appearances.

The German team leaving training at White Hart Lane under police guard on Tuesday 3 December, the day before the game.

Englands' goals in this 3-0 win were scored by
George Camsell (2) and Bastin, but it was the
presence of so many German supporters that
overshadowed events on the pitch. Cheap fares of
60 marks (£3) made it possible for 10,000 Germans
to travel to England to see the match. Close to
2,000 arrived by boat to Southampton where special
trains took them to Waterloo. The remaining 8,000
Germans travelled via Dover where special trains
were laid on. A radio broadcast carried the match
live in Germany, no doubt listened to by Hitler – he
should have heeded the warning.

There was little mention of the German salutes in
the papers the following day. There were even
reports of an Anglo-German Fellowship dinner for
sportsmen at which the main speaker, Lord Mount
Temple, said, 'If another war comes – well I must
not say what I was going to say – I hope the partners
will be changed.' He was also scathing of TUC
leaders who tried to have the fixture banned. The
irony of having the game at Tottenham's ground was
probably lost on the Germans but at least one
supporter did his bit. Earnest Wooley, who had cut
down a German flag at the ground, had his case
dismissed in court.

Part of the huge crowd watching the Christmas holiday game between Charlton and Chelsea at The Valley in 1937. Today Charlton's ground holds a little over 27,000 fans but pre-war it was the largest league ground in London, holding 75,000 fans. The East Stand (which was actually a bank, as can be seen here) was the largest in league football. For this match, which Charlton won 3-1, it was close to capacity.

The 1937 FA Cup Final

This was Sunderland's first appearance in the Wembley Cup Final, whereas Preston had been there before, as both winners and losers. This would be the first Cup Final to be televised by the British Broadcasting Corporation, although only in part. Those few people with television sets, who were in range of the BBC's transmitter at Alexandra Palace, saw Preston take the lead but Sunderland eventually won 3-1 with goals from Bobby Gurney, Eddie Burbanks and their captain Raich Carter. Of the 22 players on the pitch that day 13 of them were Scottish – a record. Among the Scots was a 23-year-old Bill Shankly.

Raich Carter, captain of Sunderland football team, holding the
FA Cup, as his victorious team return home. Sunderland beat
Preston North End 3-1 in the 1937 Cup Final.

The Queen presents the FA Cup to Raich Carter.

The 1938 FA Cup Final

Preston North End parading the FA Cup on 2 May 1938.

After the disappointment of losing to Sunderland, Preston North End was back at Wembley the following year. This time the whole match was televised meaning that 10,000 viewers saw an exciting finish as George Mutch converted a penalty in the last minute of extra-time for the Lancashire side. Thomas Woodroofe, the BBC commentator, moments before had said, 'If there's a goal scored now, I'll eat my hat', so becoming the first in a long line of TV football pundits who have been proved wrong. This was the same man who a year earlier had broadcast live from the Royal Navy's Spithead Review. Apparently he was too well entertained in the wardroom and during his commentary he kept repeating the phrase, 'the Fleet's lit up'. He was so incoherent he was taken off air after a few minutes and suspended for a week by Sir John Reith, the

Preston North End's winning team. Back row, left to right: Bill Shankly, Len Gallimore, Will Scott (trainer), Harry Holdcroft, Andy Beattie, Bob Batey. Front row: Bud Maxwell, Bobby Beattie, George Mutch, Tom Smith (captain), Dickie

Bob Hesford, Huddersfield's keeper, clears the ball.

The Preston team rest between two periods of extra time.

The Huddersfield team inspects the pitch the day before the final.

– LEGENDS –

Stanley Matthews

Stanley Matthews was the first footballer to be knighted and it happened while he was still playing. As he played until he was 50 years old that in part explains it, but it was as much to do with him being such a great ambassador. 'The Wizard of Dribble' began his career at Stoke City in 1932 aged 17 and his skill on the right wing was soon in evidence. In 1938 he asked for a transfer but when there was such a huge outcry from fans he relented and stayed. He served in the RAF during the war and played football wherever he could get a game, even turning out for a Scots XI on one occasion. In 1947 he joined Blackpool where he stayed for the next 14 years before returning to Stoke in 1961 for the last four years of his career. Ten of his final appearances for Stoke were when they had returned to the First Division, having won the Second Division title, and Matthews himself was named Footballer of the Year.

He debuted for England in 1934 and played his last game in 1957; a year earlier he had become the first ever European Footballer of the Year – aged 41! By the time he played his last game for Stoke City in February 1965 he was still good enough to set up his side's winning goal. He later claimed that, 'I retired too early'.

> *You're 32, do you think you can make it for another couple of years?*
>
> Blackpool manager Joe Smith in 1947

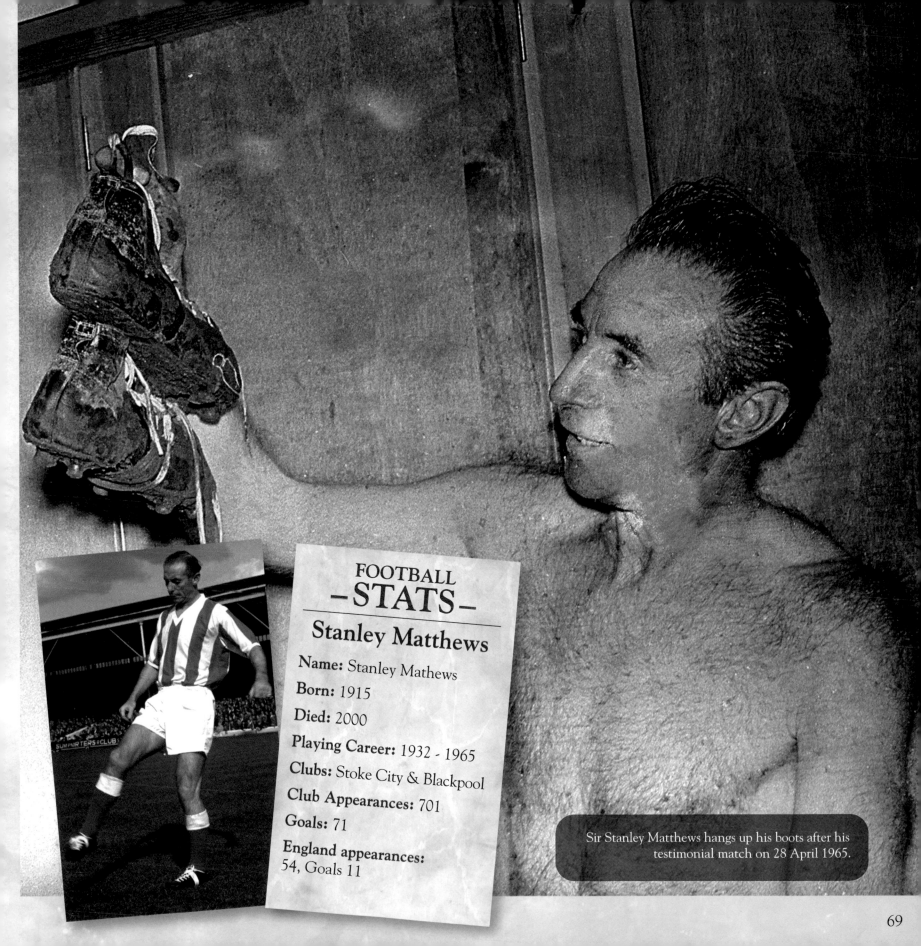

FOOTBALL
–STATS–

Stanley Matthews

Name: Stanley Mathews

Born: 1915

Died: 2000

Playing Career: 1932 - 1965

Clubs: Stoke City & Blackpool

Club Appearances: 701

Goals: 71

England appearances: 54, Goals 11

Sir Stanley Matthews hangs up his boots after his testimonial match on 28 April 1965.

The Transfer Market

In 1905 Alf Common became England's first £1,000 footballer when he went from Sunderland to Middlesbrough. It would be another eight years before that fee was doubled and it was 1928 before David Jack became the first £10,000+ player when he moved from Bolton to Arsenal for £10,800. Ten years later it was again Arsenal the big spenders when Bryn Jones joined them from Wolverhampton Wanderers. With the war looming it would be another nine years before that record was broken.

ABOVE There's always been a fascination with players and their cars. Bryn Jones outside Highbury after signing for Arsenal. Jones had been brought in after Alex James' retirement and he never really lived up to expectations; it's been said that his modesty got in his way.

TOP RIGHT Arsenal Manager, George Allison and centre half, Herbie Roberts, greeting George Drury at his arrival at Highbury from Sheffield Wednesday in March 1938. Another big Arsenal payout of £9,000.

RIGHT Arsenal's Welsh international Bryn Jones wins his duel with Bert Sproston of Spurs on his debut at Highbury – 20 August 1938.

Left to right: Cliff Bastin, Ted Drake (both Arsenal), Alf Young (Huddersfield Town), Tom Whittaker (Arsenal and England trainer), Ken Willingham (Huddersfield Town) and Eddie Hapgood (Arsenal) on board a cross-channel ferry en route to Europe for England's summer tour where they beat France and Germany and surprisingly lost to Switzerland. The match against Germany was the infamous one at which the English players gave the Nazi salute.

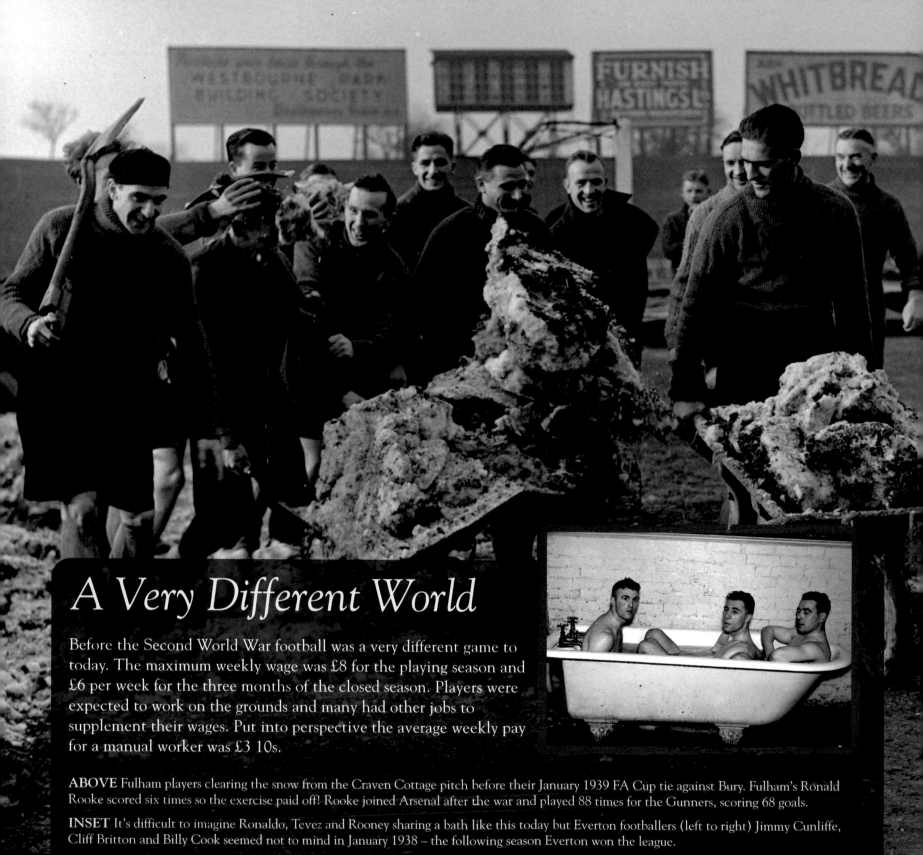

A Very Different World

Before the Second World War football was a very different game to today. The maximum weekly wage was £8 for the playing season and £6 per week for the three months of the closed season. Players were expected to work on the grounds and many had other jobs to supplement their wages. Put into perspective the average weekly pay for a manual worker was £3 10s.

ABOVE Fulham players clearing the snow from the Craven Cottage pitch before their January 1939 FA Cup tie against Bury. Fulham's Ronald Rooke scored six times so the exercise paid off! Rooke joined Arsenal after the war and played 88 times for the Gunners, scoring 68 goals.

INSET It's difficult to imagine Ronaldo, Tevez and Rooney sharing a bath like this today but Everton footballers (left to right) Jimmy Cunliffe, Cliff Britton and Billy Cook seemed not to mind in January 1938 – the following season Everton won the league.

It's Not All Glamour

Queens Park Rangers joined the Third Division South in 1920, which is where they stayed throughout the next two decades; it wouldn't be until 1948 that they would win promotion to the dizzy heights of Division Two. They played at Loftus Road in West London and toyed with having the White City as their home ground during the 1930s but lost too much money in the process.

ABOVE In January 1939 QPR were to play West Ham in a cup tie, for clubs in the lower divisions it was, just like today, their chance to earn extra gate money. Second from the right is Reg Allen who, in 1950, transferred to Manchester United for a record fee for a goalkeeper; he had been a POW in the Second World War.

TOP LEFT Twenty-one-year-old Alec Stock (left) and R. Swinton in 1938 when QPR's future manager was playing for the club. Stock became the club's manager in 1959, took them to the First Division and won the League Cup while the club was still in Division Three. With his unusual way of talking he was the inspiration for Ron Manager, Paul Whitehouse's character in The Fast Show.

LEFT Prosperous-looking William 'Billy' Birrell, the QPR manager, in August 1938; the season before Ted Vizard, the former Bolton Wanderers star replaced him.

> *Tall, powerful, agile and crafty, Tommy was the complete centre forward.*
>
> Wilf Mannion

England played Scotland at Hampden Park in April 1939 and won 2-1 with Lawton scoring the winning goal. Jimmy Carabine heads clear from Tommy Lawton as keeper Terry Dawson looks on. This was England's last international on home soil before the war.

– LEGENDS – Tommy Lawton

Unusually for a successful player from this period Tommy Lawton played for a relatively large number of clubs – six in all. His career began in 1935 when as a 16-year-old he played for Burnley. A year later, having scored 16 goals, Everton bought him to play alongside Dixie Dean who was in the twilight of his career. Between then and when war broke out Lawton scored 65 times in 87 appearances and won a place in the England side – scoring a penalty on his debut.

   After serving as a PT Instructor in the war he played for Chelsea before moving to Notts County in 1947 – a surprising move as they were in the Third Division. He stayed for four years and scored over 100 goals before becoming Brentford's player-manager in 1952. Two years later he joined Arsenal and still managed 13 goals for the Gunners despite being in his mid-30s. He went back into full-time management with Kettering Town before a spell managing Notts County that saw them relegated and Tommy Lawton retire.

Everton teammates, Joe Mercer and Tommy Lawton, who both played for England against Scotland in April 1939.

LEFT Tommy Lawton signs for Brentford in March 1952.

FOOTBALL
–STATS–

Thomas Lawton

Name: Thomas Lawton

Born: 1919 **Died:** 1996

Playing Career: 1935 - 1955

Clubs: Burnley, Everton, Chelsea, Notts County, Brentford and Arsenal

Club Appearances: 383

Goals: 235

England appearances: 23

The 1939 FA Cup Final was to be the last before war broke out a
little over four months later. Portsmouth were the surprise 4-1 winners over
Wolves, given that Pompey were in the relegation zone and Wolves were second
in Division One, and had thrashed most of their opponents on the way to the final.
Behind King George VI presenting his team is the Wolves captain, Stan Cullis, who
would later manage the club.

Football Goes To War

Soldiers watching a game shortly after the outbreak of the Second World War on 16 September 1939, but not in London where it had been banned.

Nine members of the Bolton Wanderers were all members of the Territorial Army when war broke out. In 1941 they have managed to keep together and became part of an artillery battery on the East Coast.

Despite there being no formal wartime fixtures, games were played with teams recruiting players from wherever they could. This is a game in August 1944 between Charlton and Reading at the Valley. Royal Observer Corps spotters are in position keeping a watch for the German doodlebugs, which were doing considerable damage in this area of London.

The scene outside Stamford Bridge after the gates had been closed with around 100,000 inside the ground, although how much some of them saw is debatable.

East v West in West London

On 13 November 1945 Chelsea drew 3-3 with Moscow Dynamo. The Chelsea line-up included Tommy Lawton (fifth from the right) who made his debut in this match and scored with a header. Following this game the Russians demolished Cardiff City 10-1 at Ninian Park. Moscow's next match was against Arsenal but it was an Arsenal side in name alone. With wartime strictures still very much in evidence players were drafted in from all over and as the Daily Mirror reported, 'Arsenal will be a near England eleven'. On Wednesday 21 November Moscow Dynamo beat Arsenal 4-3 – something of a shock – in fog so bad that spectators had difficulty in seeing from one end of White Hart Lane to the other – despite it being an Arsenal XI the match was played at Tottenham's ground.

BELOW A wartime game between West Ham United and Arsenal at Upton Park in August 1945. With the Hammers ground situated in East London it was inevitable that it would sustain bomb damage.

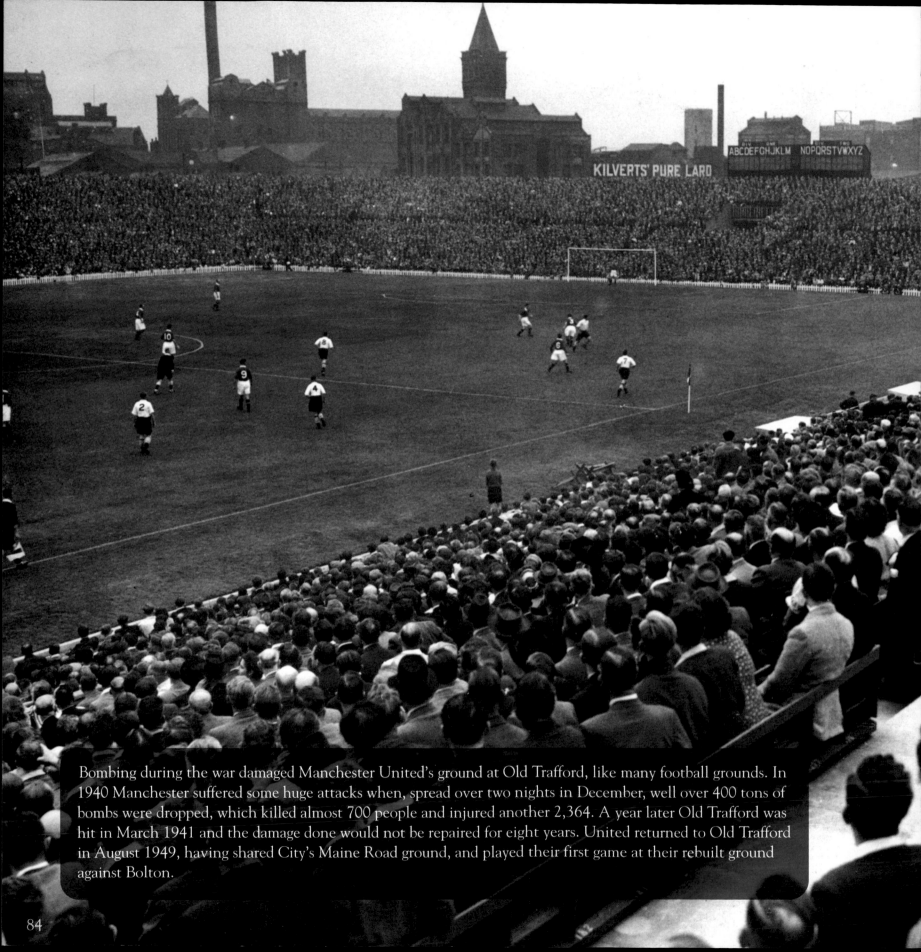

Bombing during the war damaged Manchester United's ground at Old Trafford, like many football grounds. In 1940 Manchester suffered some huge attacks when, spread over two nights in December, well over 400 tons of bombs were dropped, which killed almost 700 people and injured another 2,364. A year later Old Trafford was hit in March 1941 and the damage done would not be repaired for eight years. United returned to Old Trafford in August 1949, having shared City's Maine Road ground, and played their first game at their rebuilt ground against Bolton.

ABOVE A view of the blitzed main stand seen from Popular side.

BELOW Looking down on the new uncovered stand, which replaced the covered one, destroyed during the blitz. In the main picture part of the old stand that was undamaged is on the right.

The HARDEST GAME
1946-1967

> " *The first 90 minutes are the most important.*
>
> Robby Robson "

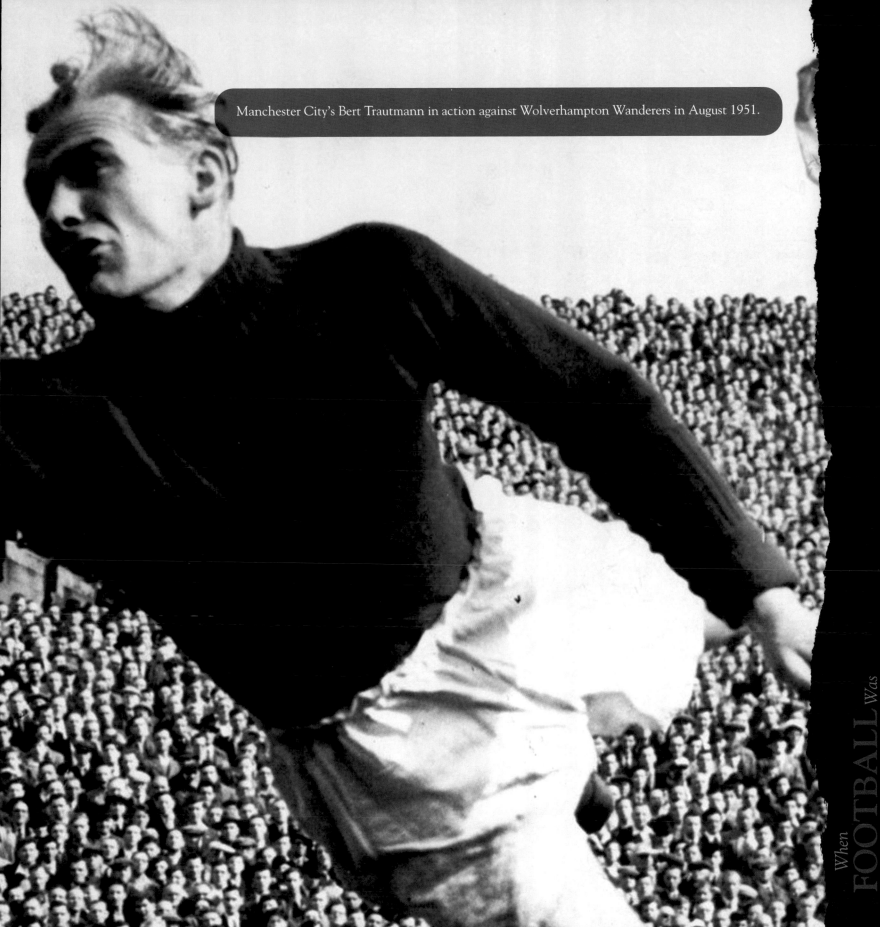

Manchester City's Bert Trautmann in action against Wolverhampton Wanderers in August 1951.

Fans at Arsenal for Cup semi-final tickets in 1950.

1946 First post-war season begins. 1947 Billy Steel moves from **Morton** to **Derby County** for £15,000. 1947 Tommy Lawton joins **Notts County** from **Chelsea** for £20,000. 1950 Leslie Compton the oldest player to win his first **England** cap aged 38. 1950 Trevor Ford moves from **Aston Villa** to **Sunderland** for £30,000. 1951 Tom Finney wins his only medal when **Preston** win the Second Division. 1951 Maximum wage £14 per week. 1953 Hungary becomes the first team to defeat **England** at Wembley. 1955 **Accrington Stanley** field a team entirely of Scottish players, the first football league side to do so. 1955 Eddie Firmani moves from **Charlton** to **Sampdoria** for £35,000. 1956 First football league game played entirely under floodlights was between **Portsmouth** and **Newcastle United**. 1957 John Charles moves from **Leeds United** to **Juventus** for £65,000. 1958 **Manchester City** score 104 goals and let in 100, they still manage to finish fifth in Division One. 1958 **Everton** install under pitch heating. 1958 Maximum wage £20 per week. 1960 **Blackpool** v **Bolton** is the first Division One game to be screened live. 1960 Jimmy Greaves of **Chelsea** the youngest player to score 100 football league goals. 1961 Denis Law joins **Torino** from **Manchester City** for £100,000. 1961 **Aston Villa** win the Football League Cup, the first club to win all three major trophies. 1961 Johnny Haynes becomes first £100 a week footballer. 1961 Terry Bly is the last player to score over 50 goals in a season. He netted 52 for **Peterborough** in Division Four. 1963 The Pools Panel met for the first time after so many matches were cancelled. 1964 The first match broadcast as Match of the Day is between **Liverpool** and **Arsenal**. 1965 **Charlton's** Keith Peacock became the first ever substitute to be used in a football league game. 1966 **Liverpool** only used 14 players when they win the League Championships. 1966 Alan Ball becomes the first £100,000 player to move between two English clubs – **Blackpool** and **Everton**.

When Bolton Wanderers played Stoke City on 9 March 1946, crowd congestion led to 33 spectators losing their lives through asphyxiation and hundreds suffering injuries. The crowd was estimated to be in excess of 85,000 people.

Southampton players being given some new tactics with the latest state of the art coaching equipment in March 1949. At this point they were well clear of their rivals at the top of Division Two but slipped to third place by the end of the season and missed out on promotion.

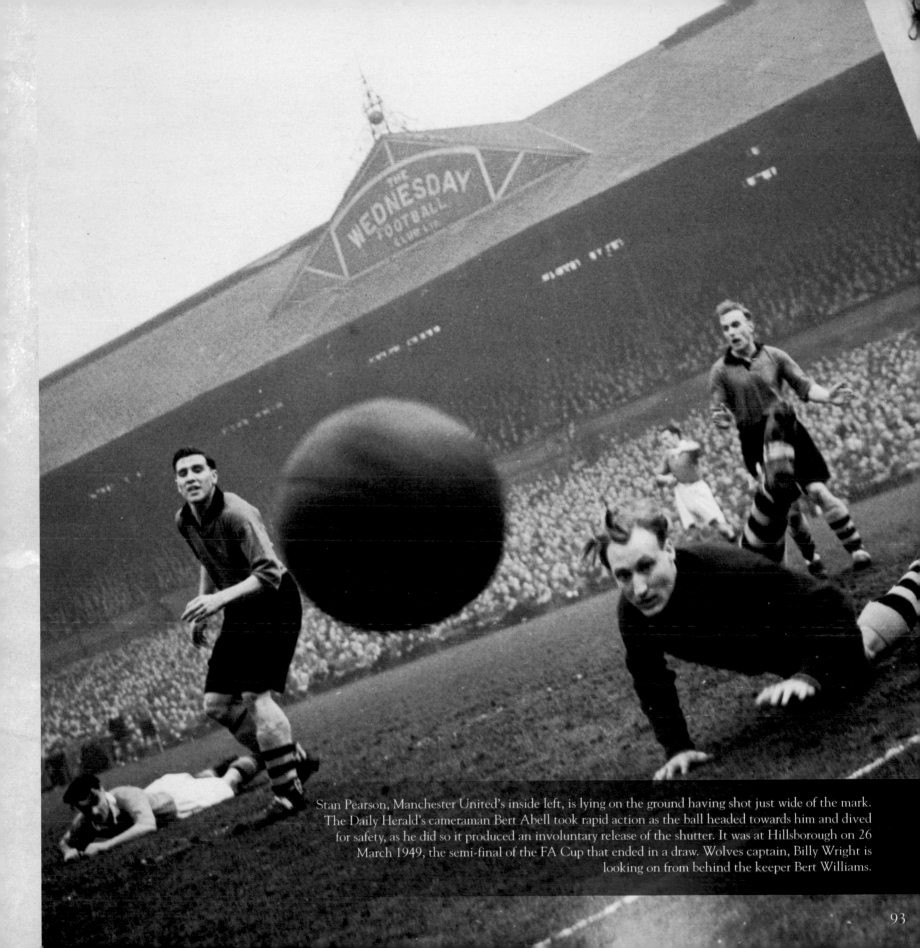

Stan Pearson, Manchester United's inside left, is lying on the ground having shot just wide of the mark. The Daily Herald's cameraman Bert Abell took rapid action as the ball headed towards him and dived for safety, as he did so it produced an involuntary release of the shutter. It was at Hillsborough on 26 March 1949, the semi-final of the FA Cup that ended in a draw. Wolves captain, Billy Wright is looking on from behind the keeper Bert Williams.

The Pools

The Football Pools started in 1923, introduced by Sir John Moores' Littlewoods company. Two years later Vernons began their rival Football Pools and then Zetters joined in this unique form of gambling in 1933, although they claimed they were not gambling as there was skill involved, putting them outside government regulation. At their peak The Pools attracted 10 million players but this has dropped dramatically since the advent of the National Lottery to around 700,000 players. The expression 'when I win the pools' became an expression of the ultimate piece of luck.

TED DRAKE **ARTHUR ELLIS** **TOM FINNEY** **TOMMY LAWTON** G

THE POOL PROMOTERS ASSOCIATION

LIST OF MATCHES — 26th JANUARY, 1963

ENGLISH LEAGUE DIV. I.   ENGLISH LEAGUE DIV. II.   ENGLISH LEAGUE D

THE EASIER SIX

BIRMINGHAM	MAN UTD	X
IPSWICH	LIVERPOOL	2
SUNDERLAND	SHEFFIELD UTD	2
NEWPORT	READING	1
SOUTH'PTON	PLYMOUTH	2
DARLINGTON	PORT VALE	2

ABOVE Former footballers Ted Drake, Arthur Ellis, Tom Finney and Tommy Lawton during the first meeting of the Pools Panel after many matches were cancelled during the big freeze in January 1963.

RIGHT Bob Smith and his Alsatian dog which helped him do his football pools.

Harry Gregg, the Manchester United keeper, saves from Lofthouse in the 1958 Cup Final.

FOOTBALL
– STATS –

Nat Lofthouse

Name: Nathanial Lofthouse

Born: 1925

Playing Career: 1941 - 1960

Clubs: Bolton Wanderers

Club Appearances: 452

Goals: 285

England appearances: 33 Goals 30

Nat Lofthouse worked as a miner at Mosley Common Pit in Lancashire during the war.

–LEGENDS– Nat Lofthouse

Nat Lofthouse was a one-club man, Bolton Wanderers, his hometown team. He played for them during the war but made his league debut against Chelsea in August 1946 and despite scoring twice ended up on the losing side. Throughout Nat's time with the club Bolton were always in Division One, including winning the FA Cup in 1958; Bolton's win against Manchester United was controversial and Lofthouse was at the centre of the controversy. United were riding a wave of sympathy following the Munich air disaster, Lofthouse scored both Bolton's goals in their 2-0 win. He shoulder-barged the United keeper, Harry Gregg, into the net for his second goal, a perfectly legitimate tactic within the laws of the game at the time, but still unpopular.

His England career was spectacular for its goal-scoring ratio, 30 goals in 33 games; including two in his debut against Yugoslavia in a 2-2 draw. An ankle injury forced his retirement in 1960, aged 35. He later worked in various capacities for Bolton including trainer, chief scout, briefly as manager and caretaker-manager twice. He ended up as President of the club he loved – a real Bolton Boy.

The 1950 World Cup

This was the first World Cup to be staged since 1938 and for a while there was a danger that it might not even go ahead at all until Brazil agreed to host the competition. With post-wartime restrictions still very much an issue, only 13 teams participated, which changed the whole way the competition was to be organised.

England went into the competition as one of the favourites but were beaten 1-0 by the USA – the most devastating result there had ever been for English football. England also lost 1-0 to Spain, which was less of a shock. The FA refused to play any of their games in the cool of the evening, under floodlights, which may have hampered England's players. Only a 2-0 victory over Chile, who hammered the USA 5-2, saw England finish as runners-up to Spain in their group. Spain went through to the final group phase, which included Brazil, Sweden and Uruguay, the eventual winners of the competition.

The England World Cup squad departing from London for Brazil on the Monday of the week in which they played Chile on the Sunday. The flight would have been 20 hours long, meaning their time for recovery and acclimatisation was very limited.

With Arsenal having beaten Liverpool 2-0 in the 1950 FA Cup Final this was the scene in their dressing room. Left to right: George Swindin (goalkeeper), Wally Barnes (left back), Alex Forbes (halfback), Les Compton (halfback), Dennis Compton (winger). Leslie Compton was one of Arsenal's longest ever serving players, joining them in 1930 and playing until 1952 – a total of 273 games. He also, like his brother, played cricket for Middlesex and the MCC. Leslie scored the equalising goal, one of only six he ever scored for Arsenal, against Chelsea in the semi-final before they then beat their London rivals in the replay, taking them to the final. In November 1950, aged 38 years and two months, Leslie Compton became the oldest player to win his first England cap.

Now this is what we call a supporter – Sheila Bowes of Driffield, Yorkshire – a Hull City supporter in January 1950 wearing the scarf she knitted with the names of all their players. Hull finished seventh in the Second Division.

Tom Finney

The man who became known as 'the Preston Plumber' was born in the street next to Preston North End's ground; he played for them for his entire career. It was a career that started later than most: he was 24, his debut delayed by the war in which he served in North Africa with the Eighth Army. Such was his impact that he got his England call-up one month after his first game for Preston. With the strictures of footballer's maximum wage legislation Finney supplemented his income and set himself up for eventual retirement by starting a plumbing business.

His loyalty to his hometown team was perhaps tested when an Italian side offered him a £10,000 signing-on fee in 1952, but he stayed put and helped Preston become runners-up in Division One that season. Five years later it was the same story and, coupled with an FA Cup defeat in 1954, it meant that Finney never won anything with his club. He was a short man but he packed a punch with both his left and right foot; he was also a great passer of the ball. When asked what was the highlight of his career he said, 'Staying with Preston'.

> " Tom Finney would have been great in any team, in any match and in any age . . . even if he had been wearing an overcoat.
>
> Bill Shankly, Finney's Preston teammate "

Finney's header hits the crossbar and rebounds with Abbes, the French keeper well beaten. It was 27 November 1957 and England won 4-0.

FOOTBALL
-STATS-

Tom Finney

Name: Thomas Finney

Born: 1922

Playing Career: 1946 - 1960

Clubs: Preston North End

Club Appearances: 433

Goals: 187

England appearances: 76, Goals 30

Tom pictured with Jimmy McIlroy, after his testimonial, taking his boots off for the last time.

Prime Minister Winston Churchill shakes hands with the Newcastle team before the 1952 FA Cup Final, introduced by their captain Joe Harvey. Newcastle won 1-0, but Arsenal were reduced to ten men after 35 minutes and then had three more injuries, leaving them with just seven fit players and three walking wounded by the end of the game.

Victorious Blackpool parade the FA Cup along the promenade on Monday 4 May 1953. The match has become known as 'The Matthews Final' after Stanley Matthews inspired his side from 3-1 down against Bolton to come back and win 4-3.

The England keeper Gil Merrick watched by Billy Wright, Harry Johnston and Alf Ramsey in November 1953 when England suffered a 6-3 defeat at the hands of Hungary. Dubbed by the press as 'The Match of the Century' in the build-up, England were 1-0 down within 90 seconds and by the 57th minute the score line was the same as it finished.

It was literally standing room only when Chelsea played Arsenal at Stamford Bridge in 1953.

It would be another four years before the first under-pitch heating was installed – at Everton's ground – so the only way to beat the freeze at Maine Road in the winter of 1953 was with braziers. The team of four Manchester City ground staff started in the morning and worked well into the night, before laying straw on the pitch to prevent it re-freezing.

–LEGENDS–

Billy Wright

Billy Wright was another one-club player; they seem like such an anachronism today. He made his debut in 1939 aged just 15 in a cup game against Notts County; like many of his generation his career was interrupted by the war. He became a PT instructor but still managed over 100 wartime appearances for both Leicester City and Wolves. He succeeded Stan Cullis as club captain and helped the club win the First Division in 1954, 1958 and 1959. Such was his fitness and freedom from injury that he only missed around 30 games during the whole of the 1950s.

His England career was equally impressive and he is among a handful of players to have gained over 100 caps. He retired after Wolves won the league in 1959 and did so without ever receiving a booking or caution during his entire playing career. He went on to manage the England youth team and in 1962 started a four-year stint as Arsenal's manager, although his tenure proved to be the least successful of any post-war Arsenal manager.

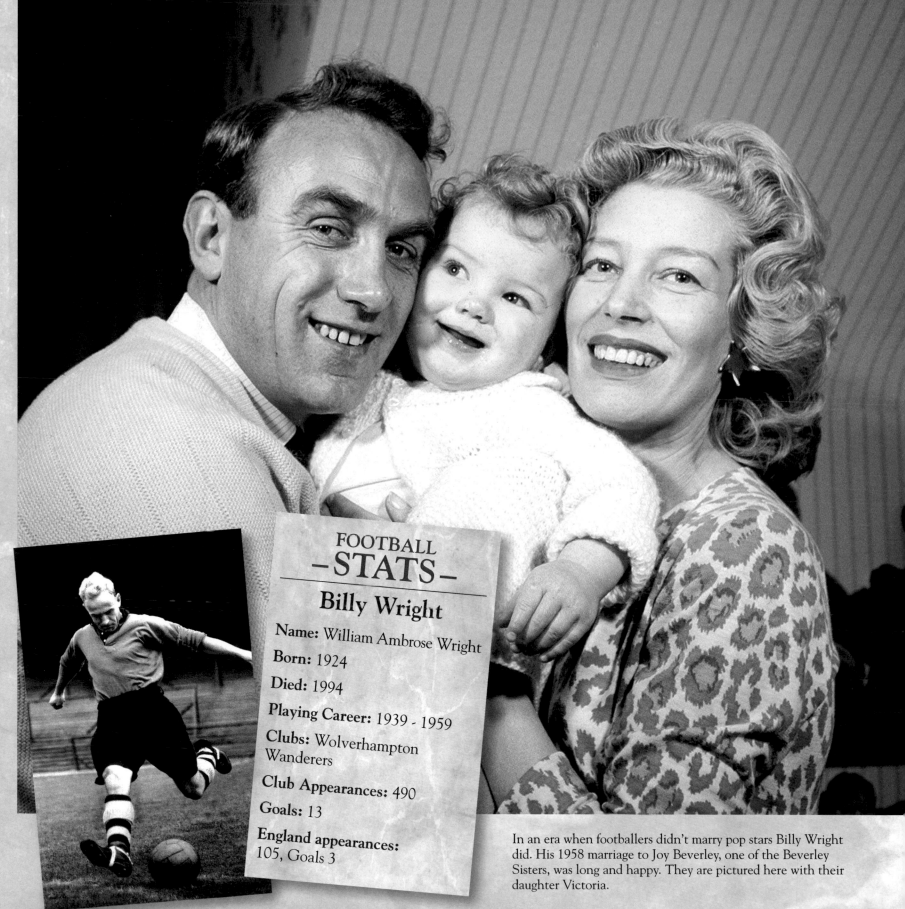

FOOTBALL
–STATS–
Billy Wright

Name: William Ambrose Wright

Born: 1924

Died: 1994

Playing Career: 1939 - 1959

Clubs: Wolverhampton Wanderers

Club Appearances: 490

Goals: 13

England appearances: 105, Goals 3

In an era when footballers didn't marry pop stars Billy Wright did. His 1958 marriage to Joy Beverley, one of the Beverley Sisters, was long and happy. They are pictured here with their daughter Victoria.

As well as the home nations matches there were games between the home nation's leagues, meaning that a Scotsman, Irishman or Welshman could technically play for this side if they played in the English Football League. Over the years it produced some interesting sides before the matches died out in the late 1970s; fringe England players were tried out in the league side before the 1960s switch that allowed 'foreign' players to play, which is why this side was all-English. The picture shows the English League team that beat the Irish League 4-2 in October 1954.

Left to right, back row: Roger Byrne (Manchester United), Nat Lofthouse (Bolton), Len Phillips (Portsmouth), Ray Wood (Manchester United), Jimmy Meadows (Manchester City), Duncan Edwards (Manchester United). Front row: Harry Hooper (West Ham), Eddie Baily (Spurs), Billy Wright (Wolves), Harry Hassall (Bolton), Billy Elliott (Sunderland).

Busby Babes, Roger Byrne and Duncan Edwards watch future Leeds United manager, Don Revie, in a Manchester derby cup tie in January 1955. City won 2-0 and Revie scored one of the goals; he played over 160 times for the club, scoring 37 goals.

Just the Ticket

In the Fifties and Sixties getting a ticket for a game was very different to today. Very few fans had a telephone, there were no credit cards; it was just good old-fashioned cash. If anyone had described the internet they would have thought you were mad. If you wanted a ticket the only option was to queue up.

Fulham fans at Craven Cottage to buy tickets for their 1958 FA Cup semi-final against Manchester United. In two hours 27,000 tickets were sold and they saw their side draw 2-2, only to lose 5-3 in the replay.

Spurs supporters queue outside White Hart Lane for tickets for their European Cup match against Dukla Prague in February 1962. Spurs won their second leg 4-1 to go through 4-2 on aggregate.

Queues of Arsenal fans ring Highbury stadium hoping to get a ticket for their 1952 FA semi-final against Chelsea – Arsenal won it and then lost the final to Newcastle United.

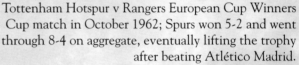

FIXTURES:

EUROPEAN CUP WINNERS CUP

TOTTENHAM HOTSPUR
v
RANGERS F.C.
WEDNESDAY, 31st OCTOBER, 1962

SALE OF GROUND TICKETS
SUNDAY 28th OCTOBER commencing 1 p.m.

NO QUEUEING BEFORE 10 A.M.

POLICE MAY DISPERSE PERSONS
CONGREGATING BEFORE THIS TIME

Crowds at Arsenal for Cup semi-final tickets in March 1950; Arsenal won through to the final where they beat Liverpool 2-0.

Tottenham Hotspur v Rangers European Cup Winners Cup match in October 1962; Spurs won 5-2 and went through 8-4 on aggregate, eventually lifting the trophy after beating Atlético Madrid.

Ticket touts outside White Hart Lane selling tickets for an FA Cup semi-final match between Luton and Norwich in March 1959. Luton won, but then lost in the final to Nottingham Forest 2-1.

In April 1955 the queue at Maine Road, Manchester, for FA Cup Final tickets, had the luxury of a mobile canteen – City lost 3-1 to Newcastle United.

Now that's what we call TRAINING

Training footballers has always been a challenge. All footballers really want to do is play football but as these pictures show the ways of getting the best out of the players has changed considerably over the years. Somehow the idea of Sir Alex Ferguson or Jose Mourinho taking his players to the beach to talk tactics just doesn't seem right.

Chelsea manager Tommy Docherty putting his players right in July 1963, following their return to the First Division, using the very latest in training techniques.

Lincoln City players in training in 1954.

Manchester City players training at Maine Road, 10 August 1950.

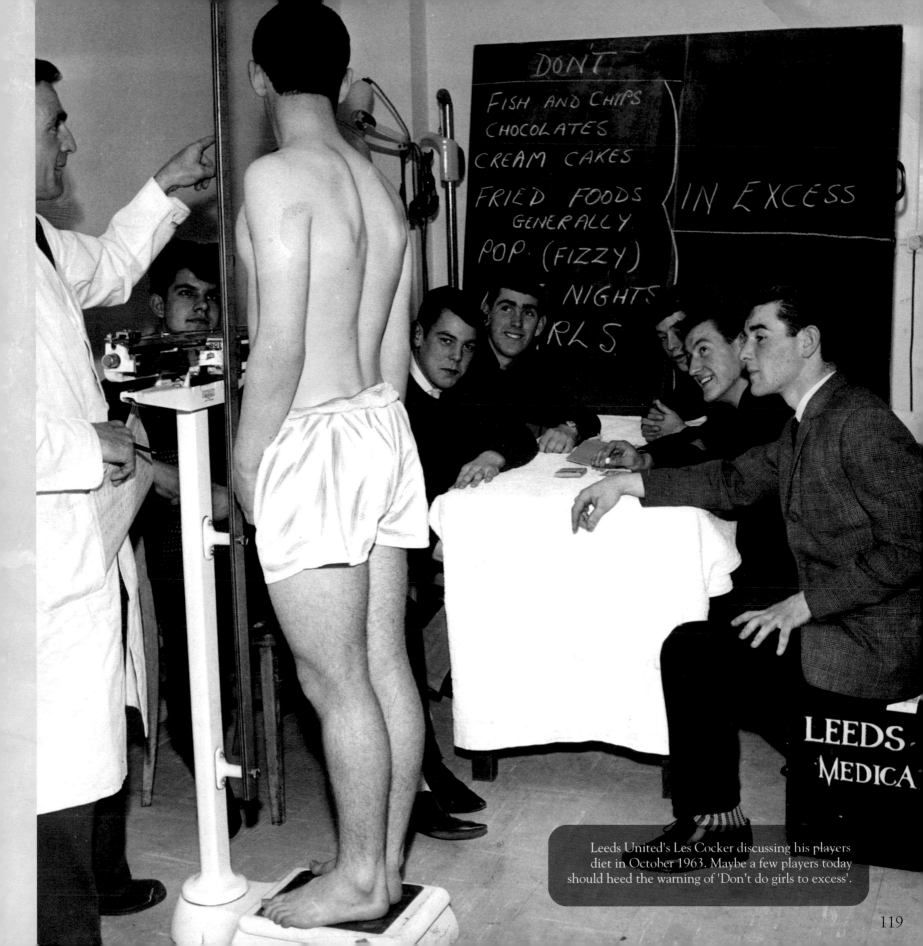

DON'T

FISH AND CHIPS
CHOCOLATES
CREAM CAKES
FRIED FOODS
GENERALLY
POP. (FIZZY)
NIGHTS
GIRLS

IN EXCESS

LEEDS
MEDICA

Leeds United's Les Cocker discussing his players
diet in October 1963. Maybe a few players today
should heed the warning of 'Don't do girls to excess'.

–LEGENDS–

Bert Trautmann

Gordon Banks' inspiration as a goalkeeper was a former German POW, paratrooper and holder of the Iron Cross, Bert Trautmann. He decided against being repatriated after the Second World War and remained in Britain, playing first for St Helen's Town. Joining Manchester City in 1949 he went on to play for them over 500 times, winning an FA Cup winner's medal against Birmingham in 1956 and dislocating five vertebrae in his neck in the match. With no substitutes allowed Trautmann, who had been knocked unconscious, played on and finished the game. Manchester City's style of play with a deep lying centre forward meant that Trautmann was called upon to throw the ball out more often than kicking it, which was very unusual for the time. But above all else it was his tremendous shot-stopping ability that made him such a brilliant goalkeeper. After his injury there was some definite loss of form but Trautmann played through it and continued to play until 1964. Although he was never picked for his country he did play for the English League team in the 1960s. After he retired he went into management, including some spells looking after some lesser footballing countries' national sides.

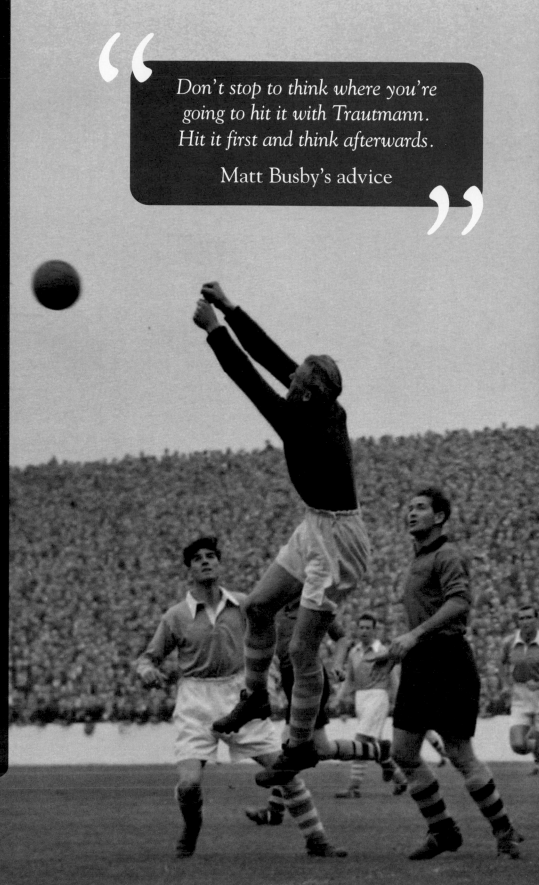

> " Don't stop to think where you're going to hit it with Trautmann. Hit it first and think afterwards.
>
> Matt Busby's advice "

Trautmann shakes hands with Prince Philip before the 1956 FA Cup Final with Birmingham City.

Bert Trautmann in 1956, with another former Manchester City keeper, Frank Swift.

FOOTBALL
-STATS-

Bert Trautmann

Name: Bernhard Carl Trautmann

Born: 1923

Playing Career: 1949 - 1964

Clubs: Manchester City

Club Appearances: 545

Goals: N/A

England appearances: None

Floodlit Football

This European Cup match between Manchester United and Athletic Bilbao at Old Trafford in February 1957 was a win – United 3-0 – sending them through 6-3 on aggregate before they lost in the semi-finals to Real Madrid.

Leicester City supporters watch a game with Bristol Rovers, which the 'Foxes' won 7-2 on their way to winning Division Two and gaining promotion back to the top flight having been relegated the previous season.

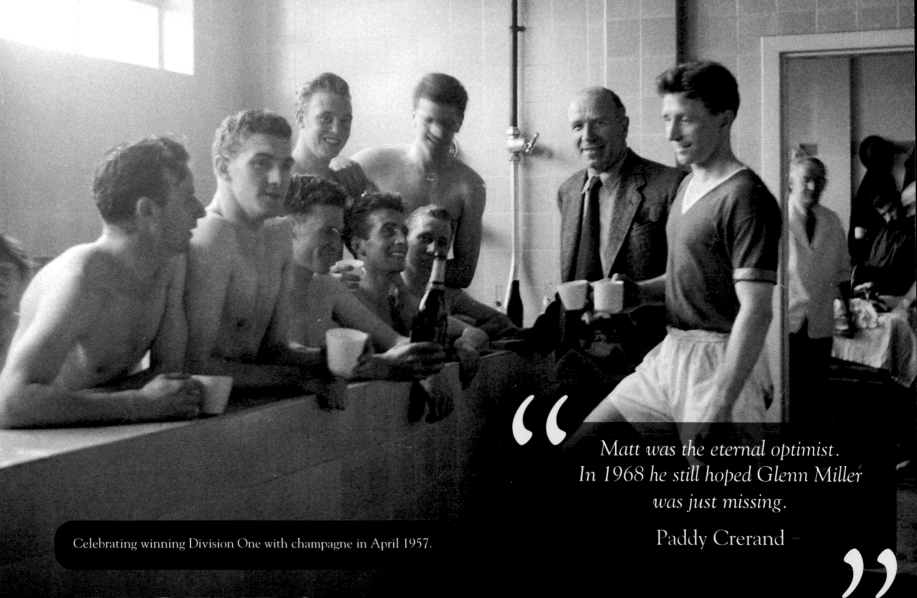

Celebrating winning Division One with champagne in April 1957.

"
*Matt was the eternal optimist.
In 1968 he still hoped Glenn Miller
was just missing.*

Paddy Crerand
"

–LEGENDS– Matt Busby

One of the longest-serving managers in modern times, Matt Busby began his playing career with his future club's great rivals, Manchester City, in 1928. Born in North Lanarkshire he won an FA Cup Winner's medal with City before being bought by Liverpool for £8,000 in 1936 – a very high fee for the time. The war cut short his league playing career but while he served in the King's Liverpool Regiment he carried on playing wherever he could get a game.

Busby almost ended up managing Liverpool in 1945 but club politics got in the way so in October that year he took over the reins at Manchester United. His influence on both the club and the modern game has been immense, his list of accomplishments huge but it was the defining tragedy of the Munich air disaster in which he almost lost his life – he twice received the last rites – that marked him out for true greatness. He came back from the huge loss of some of his best players and rebuilt his side. Under his stewardship United won the First Division title five times, the FA Cup twice, The European Cup, The Charity Shield five times and were the defeated finalists in the FA Cup twice. After his management of the club ended he became a director and later President.

One of Busby's two FA Cup wins as a manager was against Leicester City in 1963 when United won 3-1.

Sir Matt Busby and George Best in 1971 on their way back to Manchester, after his wayward star had been sent off against Chelsea.

FOOTBALL
–STATS–

Matt Busby

Name: Alexander Matthew Busby

Born: 1909

Died: 1994

Playing Career: 1928 - 1940

Clubs: Manchester City & Liverpool

Club Appearances: 344

Goals: 17

Clubs Managed: Manchester United

Management Career: 1945 - 1971

Manchester United leave Ringway Airport for their European Cup semi-final with Real Madrid in April 1957 on a BEA Ambassador; the same type of aircraft that crashed in Munich.

Munich air disaster, 1958

Having drawn 3-3 with Red Star Belgrade the Manchester United team, management and support staff were on their way home when their aircraft made a scheduled stop in Munich. Having refuelled, the aircraft made three attempts to take off and then crashed. Although pilot error was initially blamed, a build-up of slush on the runway was eventually found to be the cause – it took ten years for the pilot to be exonerated. Eight players, three members of staff, eight journalists, including the Daily Mirror's Archie Ledbrooke, two crewmembers and two passengers were killed.

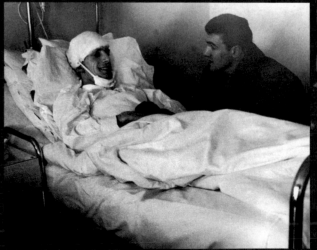

Dennis Viollet visited in Munich hospital by teammate Bill Foulkes.

Manchester United, from left to right, back row: Tom Curry (trainer, killed), Duncan Edwards (died from his injuries 15 days later), Mark Jones (killed), Ray Wood, Bobby Charlton, Bill Foulkes and manager Matt Busby. Front row: John Berry (survived but never played again), Bill Whelan (killed), Roger Byrne (killed), David Pegg (killed) and Eddie Colman (killed). Other players killed were Geoff Bent and Tommy Taylor; Jackie Blanchflower was injured and never played again.

Bobby Charlton.

Matt Busby returns to his home after the crash.

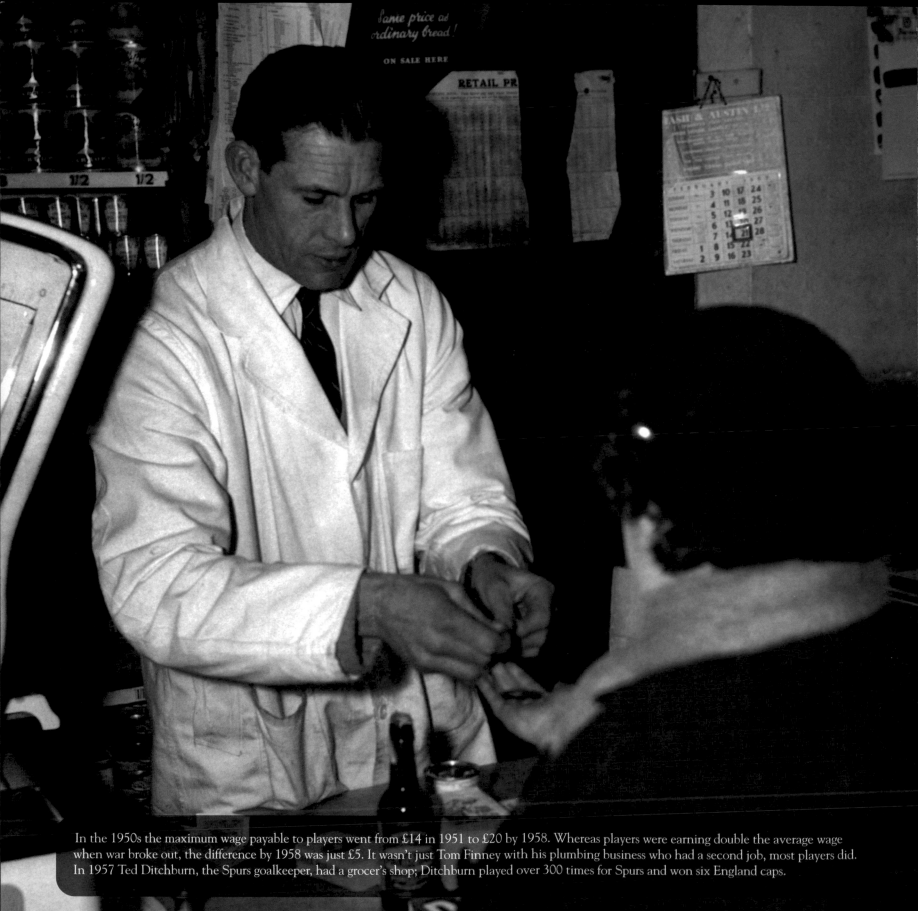

In the 1950s the maximum wage payable to players went from £14 in 1951 to £20 by 1958. Whereas players were earning double the average wage when war broke out, the difference by 1958 was just £5. It wasn't just Tom Finney with his plumbing business who had a second job, most players did. In 1957 Ted Ditchburn, the Spurs goalkeeper, had a grocer's shop; Ditchburn played over 300 times for Spurs and won six England caps.

Five Legends and Three Lions – Bobby Charlton, Billy Wright, Johnny Haynes, Tom Finney and Nat Lofthouse in training at White Hart Lane before an England match against Russia in October 1958.

–LEGENDS–

Johnny Haynes

Johnny Haynes is remembered by history as the first £100 a week footballer; his status as a legend was not for how much he was paid, but as a footballer of great vision and ability. It was following the abolition of the £20 maximum wage for footballers in 1961 that Haynes was paid what everyone considered a huge sum, at a time when the average weekly wage in Britain was £15.

Haynes was not a prolific goal scorer, although a goal every four games was no mean feet. He was much more important as a creator and was described by Pele as "best passer of the ball I've ever seen." Such was his reputation that in 1961 AC Milan offered £100,000 for his services – twice the previous transfer record – that Fulham had no hesitation in rejecting. Throughout his eighteen years playing for Fulham he never won a single winner's medal.

> " Frankly I don't think £100,000 is enough for him. He's the greatest player in the world.
> Tommy Trinder, Chairman of Fulham "

Johnny Haynes shakes hands with the Scottish Captain Eric Caldow at Hampden Park 14 April 1962. Haynes was probably thinking back to a year earlier when England thrashed Scotland 9-3 at Wembley and he scored two goals. This time Scotland won 2-0 and Caldow scored an 88th minute penalty.

FOOTBALL
–STATS–

Johnny Haynes

Name: John Norman Haynes

Born: 1934

Died: 2005

Playing Career: 1952 - 1970

Clubs: Fulham

Club Appearances: 658

Goals: 158

England appearances: 56 (1954-1962 with 22 as Captain), Goals 18

Johnny Haynes was one of the first footballers to appear in an advert – he endorsed Brylcreem, four decades before David Beckham.

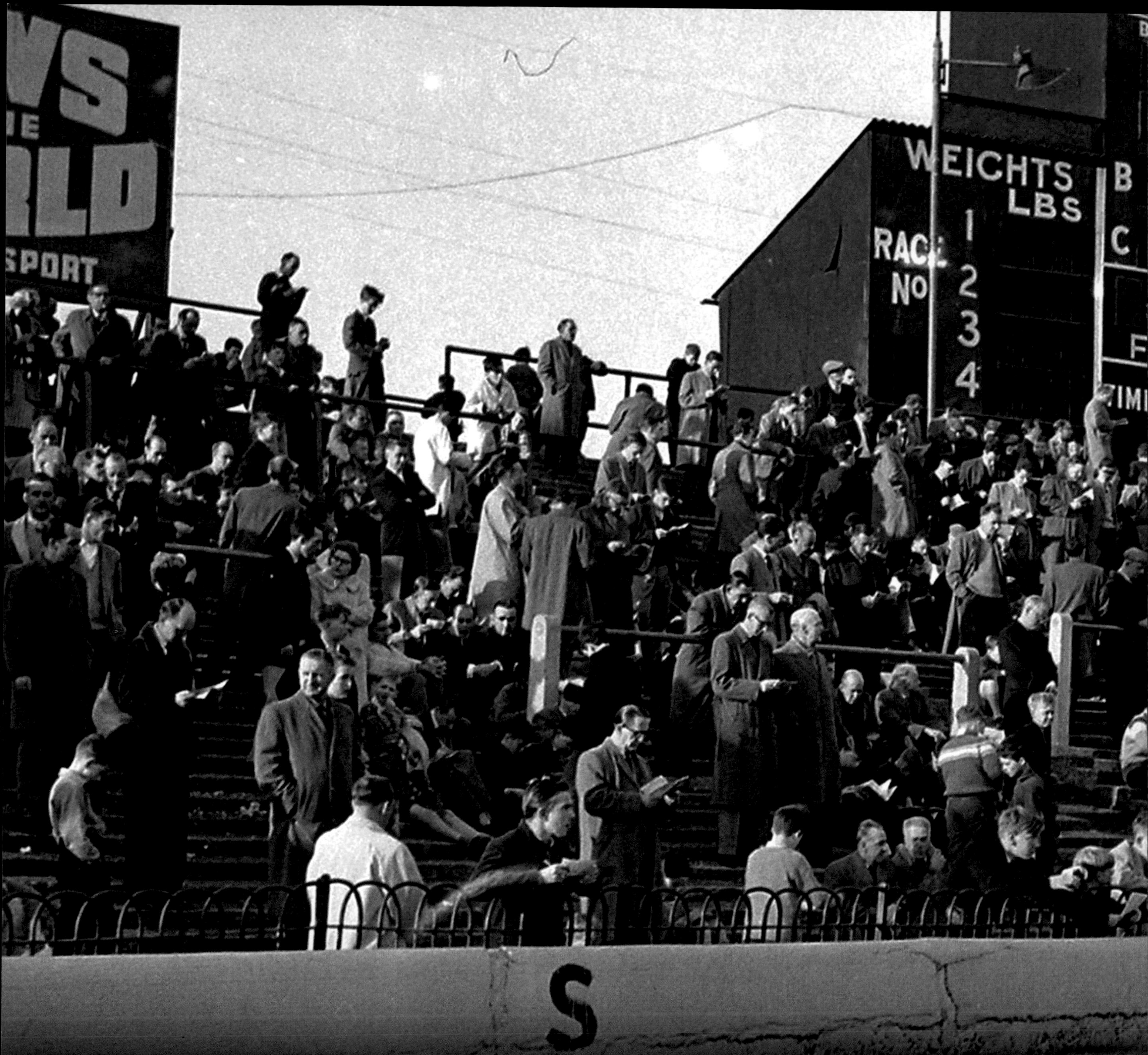
SPORT
WEIGHTS
LBS
No
1
2
3
4
S

By October 1961 Chelsea were already showing signs of meltdown and were at the foot of the table. They ended the season relegated, which led to their long-time manager Ted Drake being sacked and Tommy Docherty brought in to succeed him. Just 25,000 turned up at Stamford Bridge to see Chelsea manage a 1-1 draw with Everton. Chelsea's ground had a capacity three times that and across the city 57,000 watched Spurs beat Burnley. Stamford Bridge for many years doubled as a greyhound racing track.

"
If you don't have to drag yourself off the field exhausted after 90 minutes, you can't claim to have done your best.

Bill Nicholson
"

Tottenham Hotspur, double winning side, at White Hart Lane in March 1961.

The victorious Tottenham Hotspur team holding the European Cup Winners Cup trophy, arriving back in England after their 5-1 win over Atlético Madrid in May 1963. Front to back: Tony Marchi holding the cup, Bill Brown, Maurice Norman, Bobby Smith, John White (killed a year later, struck by lightning on a golf course), Peter Baker, Jimmy Greaves, Ron Henry and manager Bill Nicholson with thumbs up.

–LEGENDS–

Bill Nicholson

Another one-club man, both as a player and a manager, whose career was shortened by the war, which, according to Nicholson, taught him a lot about man management, that he put to good use when he took over as Spurs boss in 1958. He won the league and cup double in 1960/61; the first time it was achieved in the modern game. He won the FA Cup and the League Cup twice more, the UEFA Cup Winner's Cup, the UEFA Cup and the Charity Shield three times.

FOOTBALL –STATS–

Bill Nicholson

Name: William Nicholson

Born: 1919

Died: 2004

Playing Career: 1938 - 1954

Clubs: Tottenham Hotspur

Club Appearances: 314

Goals: 6

England appearances: 1, Goals 1

Clubs Managed: Tottenham Hotspur 1958 - 1974

Spurs beat Benfica 2-1 in the second leg of their European Cup semi-final at White Hart Lane in April 1962. However, Spurs went out 4-3 on aggregate and Benfica went on to win the cup, beating Real Madrid in the final.

Accrington Stanley, 1962

With all the glamour of teams doing the double, English teams in Europe, the end of the maximum wage stranglehold, coupled with the first £100,000 transfers it's easy to forget, just like nowadays, that there are many clubs struggling to make financial ends meet. Accrington Stanley had been a founder member of Division Three North and despite finishing as runners-up twice in that league they never made it into the Second Division, as it was only the top team that was promoted. Then, in 1960, the club was relegated into the recently formed Fourth Division – their financial difficulties began to mount.

In February 1962 the club chairman announced they owed money in unpaid transfer fees and worse was to follow as other debts to the Inland Revenue were revealed. At a creditors' meeting soon afterwards debts of £40,000 were disclosed. There seemed no other course of action but to resign from the league, which was accepted on 11 March 1962, five days after these photographs were taken. The club then joined the Lancashire Combination League, but went into liquidation in 1966. Two years later a new Accrington Stanley FC was formed and moved to a new ground; eventually in 2006 they managed to gain a place in League Two, the old Division Four. Ironically one of the clubs relegated to make way for them was Oxford United who had originally replaced the old Accrington Stanley in 1962 . . . it's a funny old game.

At one point during the game a cat stopped play by running across the Liverpool goalmouth.

The Liverpool team with their mascot and led by Ron Yeats, their captain.

The First Match of the Day

After TV's first tentative steps at filming live football in the 1930s the BBC finally got round to showing regular league football on 22 August 1964 when Match of the Day was broadcast on BBC 2. Initially it was only in the London area and the game that started it all was between Arsenal and Liverpool at Anfield; the home side won 3-2. The audience was estimated to be around 20,000, twice the number that watched the 1938 Cup Final and about half the Anfield crowd.

Gordon Wallace powers the ball past Arsenal's keeper Jim Furnell.

Chelsea's George Graham, and future Arsenal manager, in the dressing room at Stamford Bridge on 21 August 1965 with the number 12 shirt. This was the first occasion that teams were allowed a substitute. The first ever sub to be brought on was Charlton's Keith Peacock in a Second Division match against Bolton.

Northampton Town climbed out of Division Four, coming third, in 1960/61; the following season they finished eighth in Division Three. In the 1962/63 season they won the Third Division and in 1963/64 they finished a respectable mid table before finishing runners-up to Newcastle in 1964/65 – they had made it to the top flight of English football under their manager Dave Bowen. In the following season they finished next to bottom, but they were unlucky in that they finished just two points behind Fulham and lost fewer games than the five teams above them. Their problem was they just couldn't turn draws into wins, like their 1-1 draw with Spurs whose only goal was a Jimmy Greaves penalty. By the end of the 1970s Northampton finished 14th in the Fourth Division.

–LEGENDS–

Alf Ramsey

Born in Essex, Alf Ramsey started his playing career with Southampton, before moving to Spurs, making the right back position his in their strong early Fifties side. He was not the quickest of players but was always credited with being a great reader of the game, which held him in good stead when he became a manager of the unfashionable Ipswich Town in 1955.

Ramsey got Ipswich promoted from Division Three South in his second season in charge and then in 1961 they won the Second Division and were promoted to the First. Then against everyone's predictions they won the First Division title in 1962 – Ramsey's reputation was made. In 1963 he was appointed England manager, predicting that he would win the next World Cup – which of course he did. Failing to qualify for the 1974 World Cup ended Ramsey's tenure and then a spell as Birmingham City caretaker-manager brought his career to an end. Sir Alf Ramsey died in 1999 having suffered a stroke the previous year. It's fashionable in some quarters to knock Alf Ramsey but he did it where everyone else has failed.

> *You've beaten them once. Now go out and bloody beat them again.*
>
> Alf Ramsey to the England team before the 1966 World Cup Final

Alf Ramsey at White Hart Lane for Spurs against Newcastle United, November 1950.

The Ipswich team that won the First Division title in 1962. This time Scotland won 2-0 and Caldow scored an 88th minute penalty.

FOOTBALL
–STATS–

Alf Ramsey

Name: Alfred Ernest Ramsey

Born: 1920 **Died:** 1999

Playing Career: 1946 - 1955

Clubs: Southampton and Tottenham Hotspur

Club Appearances: 316

Goals: 32

England appearances: 32, Goals 3

Clubs Managed: Ipswich Town, England and Birmingham City

Management Career: 1955 - 1978

Alf Ramsey's appointment of Bobby Moore as England captain initially met with criticism, but proved inspired. Bobby lets his boss kiss the Jules Rimet trophy.

The 1966 World Cup

Roger Hunt - The missing man.

October 1966 and the England team parade their trophy in Belfast in their first game after becoming World Champions; England beat Northern Ireland 2-0.

Bobby Moore on the shoulders of his teammates; from left to right: Jack Charlton, Nobby Stiles, Gordon Banks, Alan Ball, Martin Peters, Geoff Hurst, Ray Wilson, George Cohen and Bobby Charlton. But there's a missing man, Roger Hunt, the Liverpool striker. Because of the exploits of Bobby Charlton and Geoff Hurst, Hunt's contribution is often overlooked. He scored the two goals that beat France, and one of the two goals that beat Mexico in the group stages.

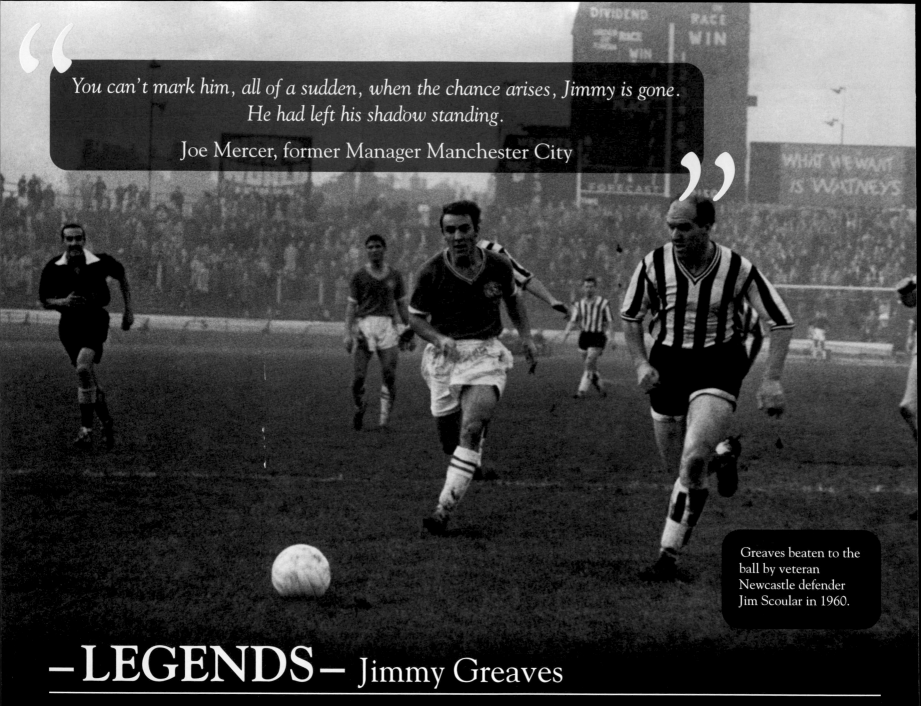

> " *You can't mark him, all of a sudden, when the chance arises, Jimmy is gone. He had left his shadow standing.*
>
> Joe Mercer, former Manager Manchester City "

Greaves beaten to the ball by veteran Newcastle defender Jim Scoular in 1960.

– LEGENDS – Jimmy Greaves

Seventeen-year-old Jimmy Greaves scored on his debut for Chelsea and for the next 15 years he rarely stopped finding the net. By 1960 he had become the youngest player ever to score 100 league goals – he wasn't even 21. He attracted interest from many clubs and joined AC Milan in Italy, but after a dozen games he was back home in London joining Spurs. Bill Nicholson signed him for £99,999 to avoid him having to deal with the pressure of being the first £100,000 footballer.

For the next nine seasons Greavsie became the most consistent striker in English football, finishing as Division One's top scorer in four of those years. He'd first been capped for England in 1959 and was a regular thereafter. In the 1966 World Cup he was injured against France and was replaced by Geoff Hurst – who knows what might have been if he hadn't been hurt? In 1970 he joined West Ham and stayed for just a year. In 1978 he made a comeback with Southern League Barnet scoring 25 goals before he really did retire to become a TV pundit, talk show host, writer and after-dinner speaker.

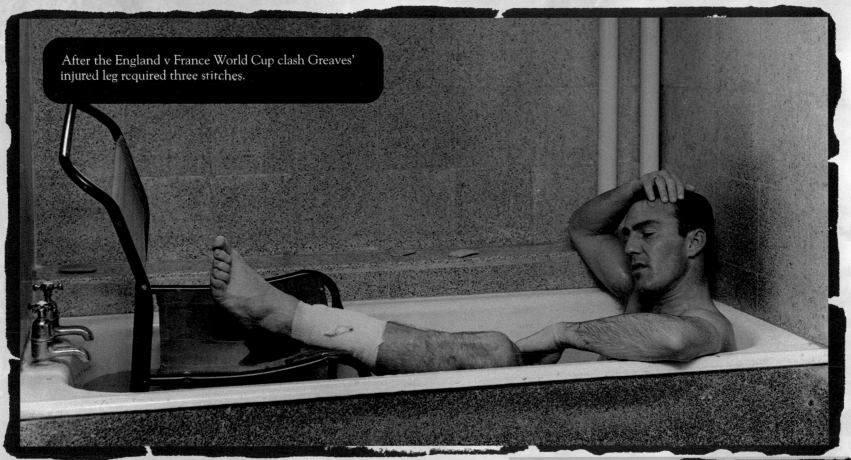

After the England v France World Cup clash Greaves' injured leg required three stitches.

FOOTBALL
–STATS–

Jimmy Greaves

Name: James Peter Greaves

Born: 1940

Playing Career: 1957 - 1979

Clubs: Chelsea, AC Milan, Tottenham Hotspur and West Ham

Club Appearances: 604

Goals: 422

England appearances: 57, Goals 44

Jimmy's West Ham debut, he scored twice against Manchester City in a 5-2 win. Behind him is Geoff Hurst and in front, Frank Lampard, the father of Chelseas' player.

Denis Law became the first player from British football to cost £100,000 when the Italian club Torino signed him from Manchester City. Less than a year later he moved to Manchester United for £115,000. In all he scored 237 goals in 409 appearances for United so it was money well spent. When he moved back to Manchester City on a free transfer Law scored against his old club in the last game of the 1973/4 season, which relegated United to Division Two. His career tally of goals was over 300, including 30 for Scotland in 55 appearances. The pictures shows Denis Law playing for United against Spurs at Old Trafford in 1967.

– LEGENDS – Bill Shankly

Such is Bill Shankly's legendary status as manager of Liverpool that many are unaware of the fact that he managed four other sides and was a great player for Preston, although the war robbed him of some of his best playing years. Born in East Ayrshire, he signed for Carlisle when he was 19 and soon transferred to Preston, where he spent the rest of his playing days. As a manager his first job was back at Carlisle, but it didn't last long because Shankly felt there was a lack of commitment from the club's board. He then learned his craft with Grimsby, Workington and Huddersfield, where he signed a young Denis Law.

When he became Liverpool manager in 1959 they were at the bottom of Division Two and far from the club they became, which was due in no small part to Shankly's uncompromising style, his passion for the game and the admiration and loyalty he instilled in his players. In 1962 Liverpool won the Second Division title and two years later the First Division – it was a remarkable transformation. Under Shankly they would win the FA Cup in 1965, the First Division in 1966 and 1973, before winning the UEFA Cup in the same year. For his swan song he won the FA Cup in 1974 and was runner-up in the title race – he would have been disappointed with that. On his retirement Shankly continued to live in the same house he and his wife had bought when they moved to Liverpool in 1959 – it's a measure of the man.

> *"There's only two teams in Liverpool: Liverpool and Liverpool Reserves."*
>
> Bill Shankly

Champagne in the dressing room after Liverpool had clinched the League Championship by beating Arsenal at Anfield in 1964. Front, left to right: Roger Hunt and Gordon Milne get their glasses topped up by Ian St John, Tommy Lawrence, Peter Thompson, Bill Shankly, Willie Stevenson, Ron Yeats; behind: Ronnie Moran, Gerry Byrne and Ian Callaghan.

FOOTBALL –STATS–

Bill Shankly

Name: William Shankly

Born: 1913

Died: 1981

Playing Career: 1932 - 1949

Clubs: Carlisle United and Preston North End

Club Appearances: 312

Goals: 13

Scotland appearances: 7

Clubs Managed: Carlisle United, Grimsby Town, Workington, Huddersfield Town and Liverpool

Management Career: 1949 - 1974

In the 1959/60 season Liverpool were in the Second Division and on 30 January 1960 played Manchester United at Anfield in the FA Cup – they lost 3-1. Come the end of the season they finished third behind Aston Villa and Cardiff.

The CHANGING GAME
1964-1984

1977 FA Cup Final, Liverpool v Manchester United.

"If God had wanted us to play football in the clouds, he'd have put grass up there.

Brian Clough
"

1968 Alan Mullery, first player to be sent off in an England shirt. **1968** Geoff Hurst scored six times in **West Ham's** 8-0 win over **Sunderland**, the last time a player achieved such a feat. **1968** Allan Clarke moves from **Fulham** to **Leicester City** for £150,000. **1969** First game broadcast on TV in colour. **1970 England** fail to defend the World Cup when they get knocked out by **Brazil**. **1970** Martin Peters joins **Spurs** for £200,000 from **West Ham**. **1972 Stoke City** win the League Cup, their first ever honour. **1972** Francis Lee scored a record 13 penalties playing for **Manchester City** in Division One. **1973** The number of clubs that are relegated or promoted increases which brings significant changes to the structure of football. **1974 Middlesbrough** won promotion to Division One with a margin of 15 points – the biggest ever. **1974** Mick Channon – First Division's top scorer despite playing for **Southampton** who were relegated. **1974** First Sunday football game. **1974** The FA scraps the difference between Amateur and Professional football. **1976 Kettering Town** becomes the first club to wear sponsorship on their shirts. **1977** Kevin Keegan joins **Hamburg** from **Liverpool** for £500,000. **1977 Wimbledon** get elected to the Fourth Division and in less than a decade they make it to Division One. **1978** Viv Anderson became the first black player to appear for **England** in an international. **1978 Nottingham Forest** went unbeaten for 42 matches. **1979 Liverpool** let in only four goals at home in the season. **1979** Trevor Francis transfers from **Birmingham** to **Nottingham Forest** for £1.18m. **1981 Liverpool** lost 2-1 to **Leicester**, their first home defeat in 85 competitive matches. **1981 QPR** first club to play on a plastic pitch. **1981** Bryan Robson costs **Manchester United** £1.5m from **West Bromwich Albion**. **1981** Clubs get three points for a win instead of two. **1981 Ipswich Town** win the UEFA Cup. **1984 Liverpool** win the League and Cup double along with the European Cup. **1984** Ray Wilkins joins **AC Milan** from **Manchester United** for £1.5m.

1977 FA Cup Final, Liverpool v Manchester United.

In December 1969 Alan Mullery of Spurs being challenged by United's George Best; a year earlier Mullery was the first player to be sent off in an England shirt in a game against Yugoslavia in Italy.

ABOVE In October 1968 West Ham United beat Sunderland 8-0 at Upton Park; Geoff Hurst heads one of his six goals past Sunderland keeper Jim Montgomery.

LEFT Anfield is the home of another Match of the Day first; the first game broadcast in colour which was between Liverpool and West Ham in November 1969. West Ham's keeper, Bobby Ferguson, dives at the feet of Liverpool winger Ian Callaghan.

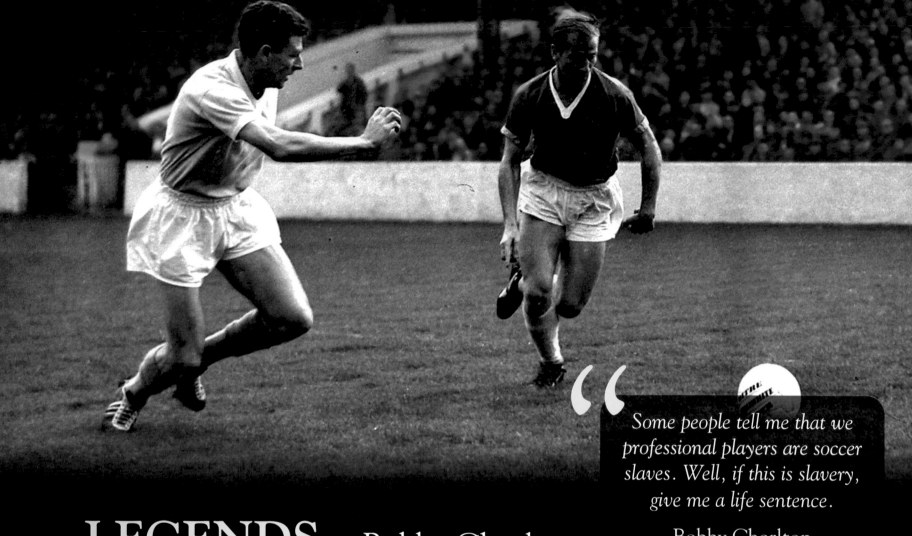

> *Some people tell me that we professional players are soccer slaves. Well, if this is slavery, give me a life sentence.*
>
> Bobby Charlton

– LEGENDS – Bobby Charlton

Like Pele, Charlton's name is synonymous with football wherever it is played – that's how iconic he is. He first played for Manchester United in 1956 having been spotted playing for East Northumberland schools, where he was born and brought up. From the start he made his presence felt and was a member of the famous Busby Babes side that was decimated at the Munich air disaster. It was just over two months after the crash that Charlton was given the first of his 106 England caps in a game against Scotland.

After he left Manchester United in 1973 he joined Preston as player-manager but found management was not for him and he retired; he later became a member of Manchester United's board. Charlton will be remembered for his wonderful shooting ability from long range, he was one of the greatest attacking mid-field players, always driving his team forward with his high work rate. With United he achieved it all. Three First Division championships, and FA Cup winner's medal, a European Cup win, four Charity Shield wins and of course a World Cup winner's medal. The complete set for the complete player.

Charlton's final league game for United was against Chelsea in April 1973. He exchanges pennants with Chelsea captain Eddie McCreadie before the kick-off at Stamford Bridge, which was in the throws of being rebuilt; United lost 1-0.

Elizabeth Charlton playing football with her three sons – Gordon aged 10, Bobby 15 and Tommy 7 – outside their home. Elizabeth's maiden name was Milburn and her four brothers all played professionally, including Leeds' Jack Milburn who should not be confused with Newcastle's Jackie Milburn; he was Bobby Charlton's mother's cousin.

FOOTBALL –STATS–

Bobby Charlton

Name: Robert Charlton

Born: 1937

Playing Career: 1956 - 1974

Clubs: Manchester United and Preston North End

Club Appearances: 642

Goals: 207

England appearances: 106, Goals 49

The Revie Revolution

When Don Revie was appointed player-manager of Leeds in March 1961 the club was lying in the lower reaches of Division Two with little expectation. Within three years Revie had got the club promoted, having built the team around Bobby Charlton's big brother, Jackie. The following season Leeds got to the FA Cup Final, but were beaten in extra time by Liverpool 2-1; the Revie Revolution was in full swing. The next season, 1964/65 and the one after, Leeds were runners-up in the First Division, the two seasons after that they were fourth and then in 1968/69 they won the First Division Championship.

Big Jack Charlton in training, August 1970.

Don Revie holds the League Championship Trophy after winning the First Division in May 1969.

Leeds was an uncompromising side in defence, epitomised by Norman Hunter who was the scourge of many a forward. Here in March 1972 West Ham United's Clyde Best attempts to go past the challenge of the man who bit many a forward's legs.

Another of Leeds' inspirational players was Billy Bremner, here he comes up against another who didn't understand the concept of giving any quarter, Tottenham's Dave MacKay, in August 1966.

The 100th FA Cup Final, 1972

Bertie Mee of Arsenal and Don Revie of Leeds lead their teams out before the start.

Leeds players celebrate Allan Clarke's winner.

Don Revie with captain Billy Bremner, holding the FA Cup after their 1-0 victory over Arsenal.

ABOVE Future Portsmouth manager Harry Redknapp, in his playing days at West Ham United, about to be tackled by Derby County's John Robson, in January 1972; Brian Clough's Derby side shocked everyone, except maybe Cloughie, by winning the title.

LEFT There was a view in October 1973 that England was still a force in international football. All that was blown away when England drew with Poland at Wembley and failed to qualify for the World Cup finals. Mick Channon crosses the ball but to no avail; his season recovered and he became the First Division's top scorer, despite playing for Southampton, who were relegated.

–LEGENDS– Gordon Banks

Gordon Banks' save against Pele in the 1970 World Cup is considered by many, including the Brazilian, to be the greatest ever. In fact it was just one of many great saves by the man who started his playing career in 1958 with Chesterfield in Division Three North after completing his National Service. He joined Leicester City in 1959 for £7,000 and went on to play almost 300 times for the Midlands club, including two FA Cup Finals where he was on the losing side on both occasions; however Leicester did win the League Cup in 1964.

Banks' tenure as England keeper began in 1963 when he played against Scotland, again at Wembley and again on the losing side, but everyone agreed Alf Ramsey had found his new keeper. His consistency for England gave the rest of the team great confidence and it was this solid foundation on which World Cup success was built. A move to Stoke followed the World Cup, his place at Leicester taken by a young Peter Shilton. Banks stayed at Stoke for five full seasons until tragedy struck when he was involved in a car crash in which he lost the sight in his right eye. Afterwards Banks went into management with Telford United but soon resigned and in 1977, for a brief spell, he returned to playing in the North American Soccer League.

Banks for Leicester saves from Chelsea at Stamford Bridge in October 1965.

FOOTBALL
–STATS–

Gordon Banks

Name: Gordon Banks

Born: 1937

Playing Career: 1958 - 1973

Clubs: Chesterfield, Leicester City and Stoke City

Club Appearances: 511

England appearances: 73

"

We lived in an era when sporting heroes were ordinary and unassuming men whose very modesty was the oxygen of dreams. And across the water, on a neighbouring island with whom we Irish had been at war for centuries I had a hero who could fly.

Don Mullen, Irish author

"

It wasn't until 20 January 1974 that the first league game took place on a Sunday. It was a Division Two match between Millwall and Fulham at the Den. With their biggest home gate of the season, 15,143 people saw Millwall's Brian Clark score the first ever goal on a Sunday.

–LEGENDS–

Bobby Moore

The most capped outfield player for England is enough to guarantee Bobby Moore's status in English football, but his captaincy of the World Cup winning side and his illustrious career at both West Ham and Fulham just enhances his reputation. Moore first played for West Ham in the 1958/59 season but became a regular in their team two years later. It was also in the 1960/61 season that he got his first England Under-23 cap; then in 1962 he went to the World Cup finals in Chile winning his first full cap against Peru in a friendly; by 1963 he was England captain – aged just 22.

In 1964 West Ham won the FA Cup, beating Preston North End, and the following year they won the UEFA Cup Winner's Cup; both matches were at Wembley and so when Moore lifted the World Cup it was three in three at the Stadium – a remarkable achievement for any footballer – he was 25 years old. Never the quickest on the pitch, or a great header of the ball, his timing and ability to read the game and his positional sense were what helped to make him great. His days at West Ham ended in early 1974 when he moved to Fulham for £25,000; he played three full seasons with the club before playing briefly in the North American Soccer League. In 1993 Moore tragically died from cancer, seven days after commentating on an England match at Wembley – he was 51.

The 1975 FA Cup Final at Wembley Stadium when Bobby Moore's Fulham lost to his old club West Ham 2-0.

FOOTBALL
–STATS–

Bobby Moore

Name: Robert Frederick Chelsea Moore

Born: 1941 **Died:** 1993

Playing Career: 1958 - 1977

Clubs: West Ham United and Fulham

Club Appearances: 668

Goals: 25

England appearances: 108, Goals 2

"

He was the supreme professional, the best I ever worked with. Without him England would never have won the World Cup.

Alf Ramsey

"

Liverpool's Graeme Souness against Frank Gray of Leeds United at Elland Road in February 1976; the Anfield side effectively replaced Leeds as the team to beat in English football.

Liverpool, 1975 - 1976

Having been runners-up in both the previous two seasons Liverpool won the First Division Championships in 1975/76 and again the following season, it was their first win in ten years. It was their new manager Bob Paisley's second season in charge, having taken over from Bill Shankly – it was just business as normal. Liverpool also won the European Cup Final in 1977 beating Borussia Mönchengladbach 3-1.

Liverpool's keeper Ray Clemence holding the Charity Shield after they beat Southampton 1-0 in August 1976.

Bob Paisley of the Liverpool FC 1977, with the European Cup and the Football League Championship Trophy during a visit to Hetton, North Yorkshire, his home town.

England at Wembley Stadium for their European Championships Qualifier match against Czechoslovakia in November 1978. Following Paul Mariner is Viv Anderson, the first black footballer to play for England.

Nottingham Forest, having won the Football League in 1977/78, so stopping Liverpool from three in a row, then beat Ipswich to win the Charity Shield.

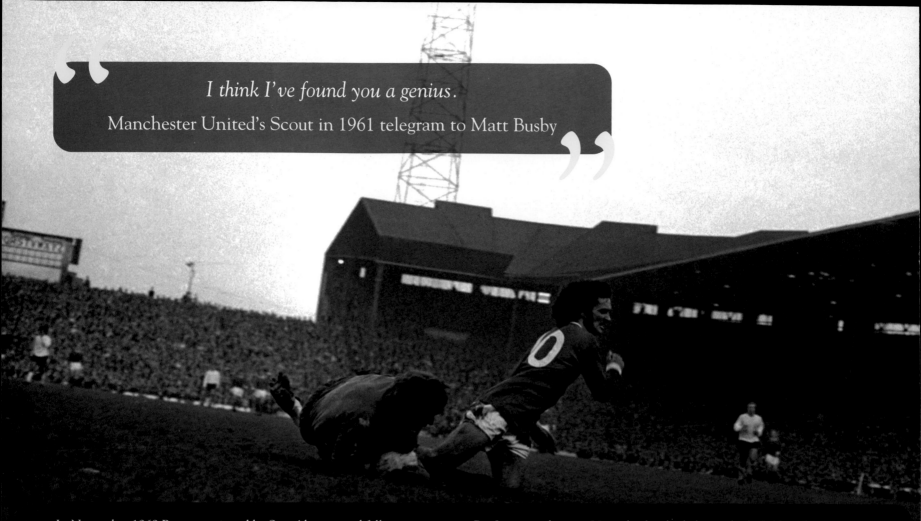

I think I've found you a genius.

Manchester United's Scout in 1961 telegram to Matt Busby

In November 1969 Best was tripped by Spurs' keeper and fellow countryman, Pat Jennings; he won United a free kick from which Bobby Charlton scored.

–LEGENDS– George Best

Football became Pop when George Best arrived on the scene, although to begin with he was just a Belfast Boy with big dreams. Having signed for United he made his debut in September 1963, aged 17. In his second season with United they won the First Division title, and Best was an integral member of the team, while not yet scoring goals as freely as he would a couple of years later. In 1966 he scored two goals in the European Cup quarter-finals, which brought him to the attention of a far wider audience; it was the beginnings of his rise to the kind of fame previously associated with pop stars. In 1966/67 United won the league and the following season, with Best scoring 28 goals, he was voted European Footballer of the Year.

It marked the zenith of his achievements and anyone lucky enough to have seen him play that season saw football of a different kind. From then on his lifestyle began to live up to the newspaper hype and while he continued to play some brilliant football and score every other game his performances were not as good as they could have been. By 1974 United had lost patience with their errant star and he was loaned out to non-league Dunstable Town. A brief resurgence with Fulham took place in 1976/77 but he was a shadow of his former self in footballing terms, if not physique. Best's international career was not as rewarding as his time with United but, to be fair, his teammates were not of the calibre to capitalise on his idiosyncratic skills.

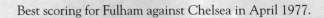
Best scoring for Fulham against Chelsea in April 1977.

FOOTBALL
–STATS–

George Best

Name: John Norman Haynes

Born: 1946 **Died:** 2005

Playing Career: 1963 - 1978

Clubs: Manchester United and Fulham

Club Appearances: 411

Goals: 147

Northern Ireland appearances:
37, Goals 9

In October 1966, Best living the dream with his girlfriend, Miss UK, Jennifer Lowe.

Liverpool, Still the Team to Beat 1978 - 1979

In the 1978/9 season, on their way to becoming First Division champions for the third time in four years. Liverpool set a record by only conceding four goals at home: QPR, Leeds United, WBA and Everton doing the honours. Liverpool won the league by eight points and their keeper Ray Clemence had 28 clean sheets. They also scored 85 goals, giving them a goal difference of almost twice their nearest rivals. In September 1978 Spurs found no way through and Liverpool's Kenny Dalgleish scores the only goal of the game, despite the attentions of Spurs Steve Perryman (centre), John Lacy (watching the action) and keeper Barry Daines.

In February 1979 Trevor Francis became Britain's first million pound player when he moved from Birmingham City to Nottingham Forest for £1.18million. It was the season that Nottingham Forest finished runners-up to Liverpool and won the European Cup, beating Malmo of Sweden 1-0 in June, having won the league the previous season; it was Francis that scored the goal. In a career that lasted 23 years from 1971 to 1994 he scored over 240 goals.

–LEGENDS–

Peter Shilton

England's most capped player earns Peter Shilton a place at the top table of English football, but so does his professionalism and his dedication to the sport for 30 years as a goalkeeper. He started at Leicester City as understudy to Gordon Banks and over 1,000 matches later he finished his career at Leyton Orient, having played at the top with Stoke, Nottingham Forest, Southampton and Derby County as well as Leicester. It was Alf Ramsey who gave Shilton his England debut in 1970, even though Leicester were playing in Division Two.

In 1989 Derby had finished fifth in Division One and Shilton was still keeping goal for England, during which time he broke Bobby Moore's England appearance record, gaining his 109th cap. It was in the third place play-off game for the 1990 World Cup that Shilton played his 125th and final international – it's a record unlikely to be beaten. A spell as player-manager for Plymouth Argyle initially started well but then turned sour. So at the age of 46 Shilton went back to playing, the following year he appeared in his 1,000th league game and then went on to play five more for Leyton Orient.

> *"What can you say about Peter Shilton? Peter Shilton is Peter Shilton, and he has been Peter Shilton since the year dot."*
>
> Bobby Robson

Future Sky TV expert Andy Gray of Everton challenges Shilton playing for Southampton in 1984 at Goodison Park.

FOOTBALL
–STATS–

Peter Shilton

Name: Peter Leslie Shilton

Born: 1949

Playing Career: 1966 - 1997

Clubs: Leicester City, Stoke City, Nottingham Forest, Southampton, Derby County, Plymouth Argyle, Bolton Wanderers and Leyton Orient

Club Appearances: 1005

Goals: 1

England appearances: 125

From left to right: Mick Channon, Kevin Keegan, Alan Ball and Peter Shilton in 1975, modelling their new England football suits.

It Pays to Advertise

In 1976 non-league Kettering Town became the first club to wear sponsorship on their shirts, when they were adorned with the name of 'Kettering Tyres' – they had no idea of what they were starting. Two years later Liverpool became the first league club to carry a sponsors' name on their shirt, but it was hard to notice because everyone was nervous that the BBC would object and so they were kept small. By 1983 everyone was doing it – some to a larger extent than others! Are we any the wiser about what some of the companies doing the sponsoring actually make or do?

A Division Two match between Bolton Wanderers and Chelsea in 1983; Bolton had a sponsor and Chelsea didn't. It wasn't down to success that Bolton had a sponsor as they were relegated to the Third Division that season; Chelsea were much higher – they were in 18th place!

Kettering Town player-manager Colin Clarke (right) with captain Sean Suddards who, by 1981, may or may not have found a more lucrative deal.

Another Division Two game, between Manchester City and Brighton and Hove Albion at Maine Road.

Manchester United's Norman Whiteside tries to go between two Brighton and Hove Albion players.

Everton and Ipswich Town in May 1983.

Stoke City in January 1983.

Liverpool's Bruce 'the Knee Trembler' Grobbelaar in December 1983.

–LEGENDS–

Bob Paisley

As someone once joked, if you cut Bill Shankly his blood would run red – well that applies ten times over to Bob Paisley. He started as a Liverpool player in 1939 and played over 250 times for the club before he retired in 1954. He became a self-taught physio and reserve team coach before becoming Bill Shankly's assistant manager. When the great man retired Bob Paisley somewhat reluctantly took over and during his tenure their success was phenomenal. They won the Football League six times, the League Cup three times, five Charity Shields, three European Cups and a UEFA Cup. Somehow or other the FA Cup escaped his grasp. After 44 years at the club Paisley retired and the day after he died in 1996 Liverpool erected the Paisley Gates to complement the Shankly Gates at Anfield.

> **"** *I've been here during the bad times too – one year we came second.* **"**
>
> Bob Paisley

Paisley holding the League Championship trophy in May 1983.

Liverpool in October 1948 with future manager Bob Paisley among their players. Back row, left to right: E. Spicer, Ray Lambert, Laurie Hughes, Bill Shepherd, Cyril Sidlow, Bill Jones, Phil Taylor, Willie Fagan, Jen Brierley, Albert Shelly (trainer). Front row: Jimmy Payne, W. Watkinson, D. McAvoy, George Kay (manager), Councillor S. Ronald Williams (chairman), Jack Balmer (captain), Cyril Done, Bob Paisley.

FOOTBALL
–STATS–
Bob Paisley

Name: Robert Paisley
Born: 1919 **Died:** 1996
Playing Career: 1939 - 1954
Clubs: Liverpool
Club Appearances: 253
Goals: 10
Clubs Managed: Liverpool
Management Career: 1974 - 1983

On 31 January 1981 Liverpool lost 2-1 to Leicester, the first home defeat in 85 competitive matches – Leicester were relegated at the end of the season.

In 1968 when he was trainer, Bob Paisley carries Emlyn Hughes off the pitch.

Dalglish in action against Swansea in 1981.

–LEGENDS– Kenny Dalglish

Kenny Dalglish's list of achievements as a player is incredible; probably no other footballer has won more winners' medals. His arrival at Liverpool, where he had had a schoolboy trial, but had been rejected, from Celtic in 1977, coincided with the phenomenal run of success at the Anfield club – Dalglish was the inspiration. He had already played over 300 times for Celtic so he was an experienced player; he had European matches and a World Cup under his belt. Once at Liverpool he again appeared in the World Cup finals and with his new club his relationship with Ian Rush created a formidable goal-scoring machine. When Joe Fagan resigned in 1985 after the Heysel Stadium disaster, Dalglish became player-manager of Liverpool. His appearances on the pitch became less but his influence on the side proved just as powerful from the dugout. He took Liverpool to three First Division championships and two FA Cup victories. He resigned on health grounds in early 1991 after the Hillsborough tragedy, which deeply affected him, although it must be said he acted magnificently throughout the aftermath. Before the year was out he was managing Blackburn, first taking them out of Division Two and three seasons later they won the Premier League. Following spells managing Newcastle and Celtic Kenny has been absent from management since 2000 – for many it's a disappointment.

Kenny on the far right with Cumbernauld United's mascot, Fiona Gibb; the club was a Celtic nursery side.

"

He crouches over the ball, legs spread and elbows poking out. Whatever angle you come in from, you're liable to find his backside in your face.

David O'Leary

"

FOOTBALL
–STATS–

Kenny Daglish

Name: Kenneth Mathicson Dalglish

Born: 1951

Playing Career: 1969 - 1990

Clubs: Celtic and Liverpool

Club Appearances: 823

Goals: 336

Scotland appearances: 102, Goals 30

Clubs Managed: Liverpool, Blackburn Rovers, Newcastle and Celtic

Management Career: 1985 - 2000

Kenny Dalglish, Alan Hansen and Graeme Souness in August 1982 after beating Spurs in the Charity Shield at Wembley.

Plastic Fantastic?

In June 1981 Queens Park Rangers laid a plastic pitch at their Loftus Road ground. Left to right: Chelsea goalkeeper Peter Barota, Barry Davis from Omniturf, the company that made the new surface, Terry Venables, who had become QPR's manager during the previous season and Mike Leach of Chelsea inspect the newly-laid turf. The first match on the new surface was on 1 September against Luton; ironically they became the second club to install a plastic playing surface.

Watford are '⬛n Song' – 198⬛

Elton John had been a lifelong Watford fan and when he bought the club in 1976/77, installing Graham Taylor as the club's manager, they were languishing in Division Four. Come the 1982/83 season little old Watford were competing with the best clubs in England having gained promotion all the way through the divisions to the top flight. If that wasn't enough they actually managed to finish second behind Liverpool. Although they trailed the Anfield side by 11 points Watford were a point ahead of Manchester United, despite losing to them at Old Trafford in one of the last games of the season. Luther Blissett was one of the stars of the Watford side and the First Division's top scorer is challenged by United's Paul McGrath.

Spurs snapped up Ossie Ardilles, along with Ricky Villa, after Argentina won the World Cup in 1978. They both become firm favourites at White Hart Lane until the Falklands conflict made them persona non grata. Spurs loaned Ardilles to Paris St Germain but by January 1983 it was felt safe for him to return to English football. His rehabilitation began in front of 500 fans in a reserve game against Luton.

In April 1984 future England manager Kevin Keegan, who had started his career as a player with Scunthorpe United in 1968, played his last match for Newcastle United, helping them gain promotion to Division One, having been absent for six seasons. In between he'd played for Liverpool, Hamburg and Southampton; after retiring he went into management with Newcastle, Fulham, and Manchester City.

Lawrie McMenemy as Southampton manager did a fantastic job with one of the less glamorous English teams. He took them to the FA Cup Final in 1976 where they beat Manchester United and two years later he took the team up to Division One. In the 1983/84 season Southampton finished as runners-up to Liverpool. That same season they were beaten FA Cup semi-finalists, having disposed of Portsmouth in this Fifth Round tie at Fratton Park. Mark Wright, the Southampton No. 6, tussles with Mark Hateley, watched by Steve Moran, Southampton's top scorer that season.

Brian Clough, with assistant Peter Taylor, watching Nottingham Forest in September 1977.

–LEGENDS– Brian Clough

Brian Clough's achievements as a manager are the very stuff of legend; his uncompromising style, wit and candor made him as many enemies as he had friends and it all helps us to forget what a great goalscorer he was. While it's easy to say they were mostly in Division Two he still scored nearly a goal a game in 274 appearances before his career was effectively ended by injury in 1962. Clough took up management with Hartlepool United in 1965, having had a brief three game return to Sunderland's first team; with him at Hartlepool was the man who would become his long-time assistant – Peter Taylor.

In 1967 the pair took over at Derby County and gained them promotion to Division One two years later; by 1970 they managed a fourth place in the top flight – a remarkable turnaround for an unfashionable club that had spent years flirting with relegation to Division Three. The following season they won the league – an even more remarkable achievement. The duo fell out with the Derby board, resigning in 1973 and went to manage Brighton – it was far from their finest hour. Clough on his own managed Leeds before being sacked after 44 days. In 1975 Clough became manager of Nottingham Forest and was soon rejoined by Taylor. The two of them performed a minor miracle taking Forest out of Division Two before winning the First Division in 1978; they also won the League Cup four times and the European Cup Winner's Cup twice.

> " *I certainly wouldn't say I'm the best manager in the business, but I'm in the top one.*
>
> Brian Clough "

FOOTBALL
–STATS–

Brian Clough

Name: Brian Howard Clough

Born: 1935 **Died:** 2004

Playing Career: 1955 - 1964

Clubs: Middlesbrough and Sunderland

Club Appearances: 274

Goals: 251

England appearances: 2

Clubs Managed: Hartlepool United, Derby County, Brighton and Hove Albion, Leeds United and Nottingham Forest

Management Career: 1965 - 1993

Clough comes out for the second half on his return debut for Sunderland at Roker Park in August 1964; he only played two more games before he retired.

The SIMPLEST GAME
1985-1992

Liverpool's John Barnes, watched by Norwich City's Ian Culverhouse, in 1990.

"

Nearly everything possible had been done to spoil the game: the heavy financial interest; the absurd transfer and player-selling system; the lack of any birth or residential qualifications; the absurd publicity given to every feature of it by the press; the monstrous partisanships of the crowds.

J.B Priestley in 1933

"

1985 Kevin Moran of **Manchester United** is the first player to be sent off in an FA Cup Final. 1985 **Preston** and **Burnley**, two of the original members of the football league, dropped into the Fourth Division for the first time. 1985 The **Heysel** stadium riots damage English football for years. 1986 **Wolves** go from Division One in 1984 to Division Three in 1986. **1986** Mark Hughes moves from **Manchester United** to **Barcelona** for £2.3m. 1986 The 'Hand of God' further punishes English football. 1987 Ian Rush leaves **Liverpool** for **Juventus** for £3.2m. 1987 **Coventry City** win the FA Cup, their first major honour. 1988 **Luton Town** beat **Arsenal** in the League Cup Final to secure their first major honour. 1988 **Liverpool** win the First Division losing only two games in the season. 1989 Alan Shearer scores a hat trick, aged 17, on his First Division debut for **Southampton**. **1989** Peter Shilton becomes most capped England player. 1989 Chris Waddle moves from **Tottenham Hotspur** to **Marseilles** for £4.25m. 1989 Five penalties in one game between **Crystal Palace** and **Brighton** in Division Two. 1989 Nigel Martyn becomes first £1m goalkeeper when he signs for **Crystal Palace** from **Bristol Rovers**. **1989 Arsenal** win the First Division, denying a **Liverpool** club an eighth successive title, only losing one game all season. 1991 David Platt joins **Bari** from **Aston Villa** for £5.5m. **1991** Dean Saunders moves from **Derby County** to **Liverpool** for £2.9m. 1992 **Wrexham** knock **Arsenal**, the reigning champions, out of the FA Cup having finished bottom of the league in the previous season. 1992 Paul Gascoigne joins **Lazio** from **Spurs** for £5.5m. 1992 The FA Premier League was formed.

Manchester United fans at the European Cup Winners Cup Final in Rotterdam in 1991; United beat Barcelona 2-1.

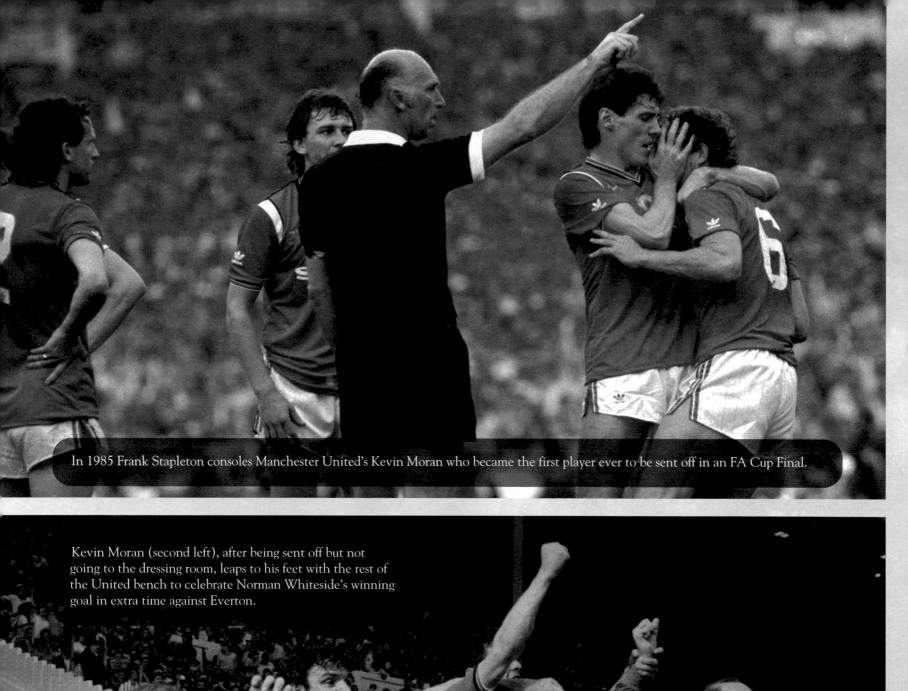

In 1985 Frank Stapleton consoles Manchester United's Kevin Moran who became the first player ever to be sent off in an FA Cup Final.

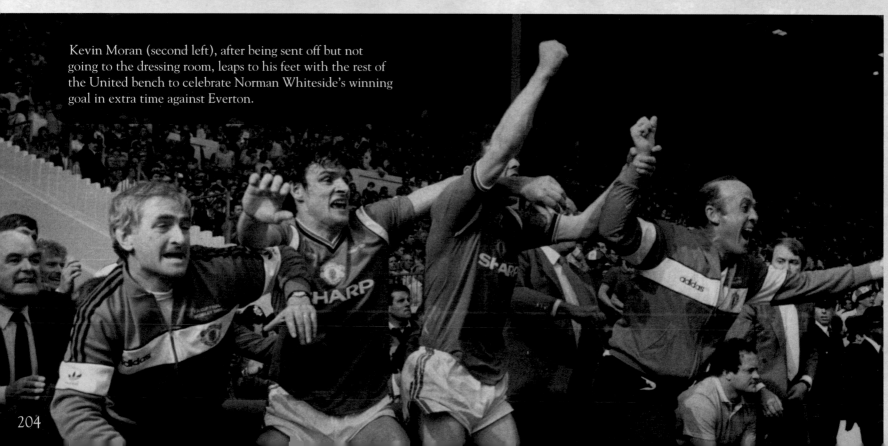

Kevin Moran (second left), after being sent off but not going to the dressing room, leaps to his feet with the rest of the United bench to celebrate Norman Whiteside's winning goal in extra time against Everton.

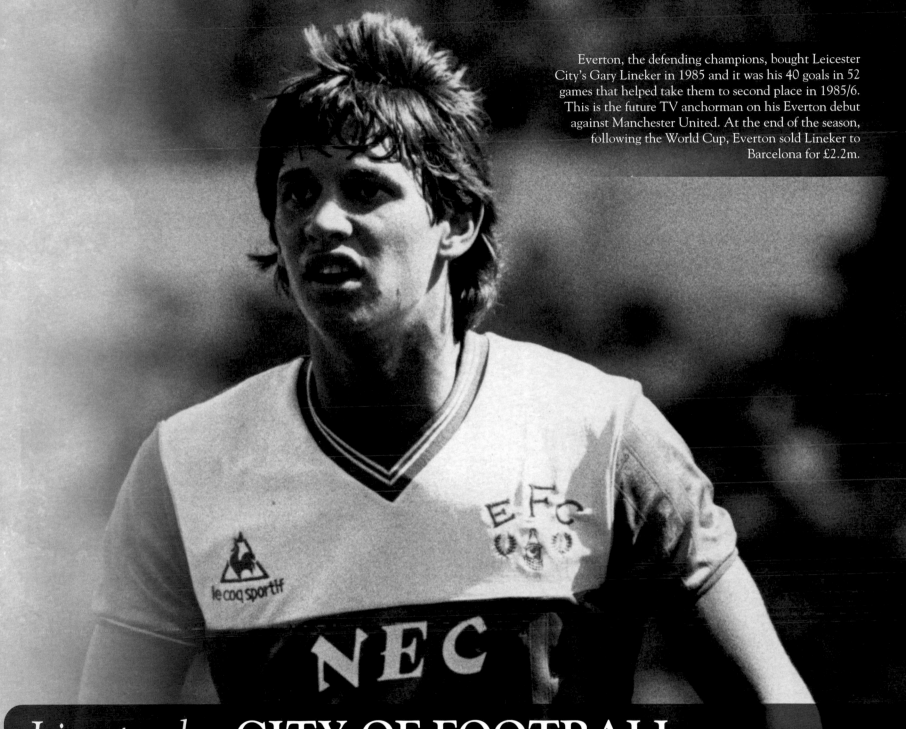

Everton, the defending champions, bought Leicester City's Gary Lineker in 1985 and it was his 40 goals in 52 games that helped take them to second place in 1985/6. This is the future TV anchorman on his Everton debut against Manchester United. At the end of the season, following the World Cup, Everton sold Lineker to Barcelona for £2.2m.

Liverpool – CITY OF FOOTBALL

Between 1975 and 1990 only three teams, other than one from Liverpool, won the First Division title; while Liverpool were rampant Everton picked up two titles – 1984/5 and 1986/7 and the season in between they were runners-up to their old rivals. In their first winning season Everton won by 13 points scoring 88 goals in the process. In the 1986/7 season, Everton's final campaign under Howard Kendell's management, they were again very strong winning by a nine point margin; the previous season they had only lost out to Liverpool by two points.

Manchester City had been in the top flight for 20 years, while Charlton had only just been promoted; their first league meeting at Maine Road ended in a victory for City. By the end of the season City were on their way down to the Second Division and Charlton only managed to retain their top flight status by beating Leeds in the play-off between the fourth from bottom Division One side and the winner of the Division Two play-offs. Here Tony Curbishley, who would manage Charlton from 1991 until 2006, clears the danger.

With their new state-of-the-art stadium Arsenal's days of having to clear snow off the terracing are long gone. Highbury in January 1967.

March 1987 and Watford's John Barnes celebrates his second goal against Arsenal, along with teammate Mark Falco. After scoring 83 goals in almost 300 appearances for Watford Barnes joined Liverpool for £900,000.

Paul Gascoigne – Gazza – always the joker, although in 1988 when he came up against Vinnie Jones, leader of Wimbledon's Crazy Gang, he probably didn't get the joke.

1988 FA Cup Final

When 'The Crazy Gang' took on Liverpool in the 1988 FA Cup Final at Wembley no one gave them a chance.
It was only a decade earlier that Wimbledon had actually made it out of non-league football and into the Fourth Division.
A goal from Laurie Sanchez won them their FA Cup winner's medals, because, despite how it looks, Dave Beeasant saved this penalty and Wimbledon won 1-0.

An eighth Football League title win in a row for a Liverpool club was denied by the last kick of the game between Arsenal and Liverpool, deep into injury time in May 1989. Arsenal had travelled north, three points behind Liverpool, knowing they had to win by two clear goals to knock Liverpool off the top spot. Alan Smith scored first and Michael Thomas achieved what seemed an unlikely end to the season in the 91st minute. It also prevented Liverpool from clinching their second league and cup double in a consecutive season.

In 1990 Liverpool were going for their third consecutive FA Cup Final appearance when they faced Crystal Palace at Villa Park. Liverpool, having already beaten the Palace twice during the season, once 9-0, started as firm favourites. Ian Rush scored Liverpool's opening goal and at half-time they were 1-0 up, come full-time it was 3-3; Palace won with an extra time winner.

It was just another day in the long history of Manchester United.

Sir Alex Ferguson after a particularly heavy defeat

Alex Ferguson and assistant Archie Knox with the European Cup Winners Cup at Aberdeen's ground, after winning in Gothenburg in May 1983.

–LEGENDS– Alex Ferguson

Because Alex Ferguson has been managing Manchester United for over 20 years it's sometimes easy to forget everything he's achieved. As a player he started out as an amateur for Queens Park while working in the Glasgow shipyards; it wasn't until he moved to Dunfermline six years later that he turned professional. By 1966 he was the Scottish League's top scorer and then joined Rangers for a record fee between two Scottish clubs. Having been blamed for a goal in the 1969 Scottish Cup Final Ferguson had a falling out with Rangers and moved to Falkirk before finishing his career at Ayr United.

He immediately became manager of East Stirlingshire – a part-time job – before moving to St Mirren soon afterwards. He took them from being Second Division also-rans to winning the division in two seasons and took the club to the Premier Division, but a fall out with the club saw him switch to Aberdeen in 1978. By the end of the 1980 season Aberdeen won the Scottish League Championship breaking a 15 year 'old firm' stranglehold. In 1983 Aberdeen won the European Cup Winner's Cup and more domestic success followed, as well as a spell as the Scotland manager, before Ferguson joined Manchester United at the end of 1986. Any previous success has been dwarfed by his achievement at Manchester United. He's broken almost every English club record and created many more. He has become the most successful manager in the history of British club football and given the current state of the game it's a record that may well never be broken.

Scotland international football squad in 1967. Back row, left to right: Alex Ferguson, Dave Smith, Pat Stanton, Bobby Ferguson, Jim Cruickshank, Billy McNeill, Tommy Gemmell. Front row: John Greig, Peter Cormack, Willie Henderson, John Clark, Jimmy Wilson, Steve Chalmers, Bobby Lennox. Alex Ferguson never actually got selected to play for his country.

FOOTBALL
– STATS –

Alex Ferguson

Name: Alexander Chapman Ferguson

Born: 1941

Playing Career: 1957 - 1974

Clubs: Queen's Park, St Johnstone, Dunfermline Athletic, Rangers, Falkirk and Ayr United

Club Appearances: 327

Goals: 167

Clubs Managed: East Stirlingshire, St Mirren, Aberdeen, Scotland and Manchester United

Management Career: 1974 -

Alex Ferguson in 1982 studying an atlas as Aberdeen embarked upon the European Cup Winner's campaign in which they eventually triumphed.

Football Dreams

Oscar Wilde was probably not much bothered by football but he did urge us to 'expect the unexpected' – which is something that has often occurred, not just in the modern game, but from when football was first organised into an association back in 1863; the playwright, poet and novelist was nine years old. The unexpected is what helps to make football what it is. Dreams do come true, even if with today's multi-million pound super sides it does mean you have to dream a little harder.

Back in 1992 Arsenal were the reigning football league champions; they had won the League quite comfortably the season before, having only been beaten once. When the third round draw for the FA Cup was announced and Wrexham came out of the hat as a home tie against Arsenal the Welsh club probably thought – a good little earner. Any ambition would have been tempered by knowing they had finished bottom of the Fourth Division the previous season. But for a few dreams did come true – Wrexham won 2-1! Come the fourth round and Wrexham were drawn away to West Ham, not the once mighty Hammers, as they were propping up the First Division. The Welsh side held them to a 2-2 draw before losing in the replay 1-0. Every dream comes to an end. . . .

Steve Watkins celebrates with 37-year-old Micky Thomas (right) who scored the first Wrexham goal against the Gunners. Thomas by this time had been playing for 21 seasons, under 21 managers at 11 different clubs.

Frenchman Eric Cantonas' debut for Manchester United in 1992 was against their old rivals Manchester City. Cantona was among a comparatively small number of foreign players plying their trade in Britain – he would prove to be one of the most charismatic and exciting footballers of his generation. From less than one in ten players in the Premiership coming from outside the British Isles back in 1992 the balance has swung the other way. In years to come maybe there will even be a book that has a picture of the last British-born player to start a Premier League match.

" *When the seagulls follow the trawler, it is because they think sardines will be thrown into the sea.*

Eric Cantona

"

"A pictures worth a thousand words", so the old saying goes.
If it's true, and who are we to argue, then this book would be closer to half a million words
than the twenty five thousand words that it is. If it were it would be far less interesting.
So it is with thanks and with the greatest respect we acknowledge the man who took 'em.

Mirror / Sunday Mirror / People

Horace Grant (Most probably our first sports photographer), Peter Cook (1966 World Cup),
Albert Cooper, Michael Fresco, Monty Fresco, Kent Gavin, W.E.G. Heanly, Harry Ormesher, Bradley Ormesher,
John Varley (1966 World Cup), Arthur Sidey, Bill Turner, Tom Buist (1966 World Cup) and Roland Hicklin

Daily Herald

Bert Abell, Edward Malindine, George Roper, Harold Tomlin and Peter Ralph

Photographic Research – John Mead, Vito Inglese, Mel Knight & Alex Waters

For T.P